# Buffalo Bill — His Life & Legend
Museum Edition
by O.J. Seiden

---

Stan Zaminski
historical editor

Standing Stone Series

Cover: Buffalo Bill and Isham
by Robert Lindneoy

Acknowledgments:

This book could not have been written without the cooperation of the Buffalo Bill Memorial Museum atop Lookout Mountain. A special thanks must go to Stan Zamonski, curator of the museum, for his help in editing for historical accuracy. It was no small job separating myth from fact in the life of Buffalo Bill Cody. The rare photographs found in this book are all from the collection of the museum, and many have never been published before.

Copyright 1981
by Othniel J. Seiden
All rights reserved
Library of Congress Catalogue
Card number 81-50065
ISBN 0-937050-15-6
Made in U.S.A.

Dedicated to all the people who have contributed to the preservation of the memory of Buffalo Bill and our heritage in the old West . . . .

Buffalo Bill - His Story and Memorial

by O.J. Seiden

# Buffalo Bill: The Living Legend . . . Scout, Hunter, Showman

Too many people, over the years, have thought Buffalo Bill a product of publicity, fiction, and "B" movies. Actually he was a giant of his times. The "real" Buffalo Bill Cody was far more remarkable than the people who exploit his name make him out to be. He was far more fascinating than any fiction writer's imagination.

William Frederick Cody was born on February 26, 1846, in Le Claire, Scott County, Iowa. He was the fourth of eight children born to his parents, Mary Ann Leacock Cody and Isaac Cody. Two older sisters, Martha and Julia, and an older brother Samuel, welcomed the newborn. Three more girls followed, Eliza, Helen and May, before the youngest brother, Charlie, completed the group. His mother was a well educated woman, and from the day of his birth, was convinced that *Will* would grow up to be President of the United States. His father, Isaac, was a restless man, energetic and ambitious. He found little to his liking in the East, and settled in Iowa when he passed through on his way to California. The Cody family was happy living in

Cody home in Iowa, where Bill spent his first years.

Le Claire. They had a fine two story frame home, roomy and comfortable. They raised much of their food and were relatively carefree. The children learned from their parents and from their environs. Will was an especially bright child and picked everything up quickly. He seemed to have his father's restless, ambitious temperament, and his mother's wit and intelligence.

William at
18 months.

When Will was six years old, his older brother, Samuel, died as a result of a fall from a horse. Their mother went into deep depression over the loss so Isaac decided to move away from the place that held so many reminders for her.

Young Billy —
Cody at age four.

The journey would have a lasting effect on little Will. From the outset he rode alongside on his pony, playing at being wagon master, guide, Indian scout, and sometimes even a renegade Indian stalking the "paleface" pioneer family.

The trip took a full month and ended in Weston, Missouri where his uncle, Elijah Cody, kept a general store, supplying the residents as well as wagons traveling West. Outfitting settlers and pioneers was lucrative business in those times. After a short stay, the family turned West and crossed into Kansas. Little did they realize that the future held even more dramatic changes and tragedy for them.

## The Cody's Settle in Kansas

As they approached Fort Leavenworth, young Will noticed his world changing. He began seeing westerners in buckskins, and Indians everywhere. Men were armed. Military personnel were very visible. The fort itself was a beehive of activity. There was a sense of danger—to young Will an excitement. This was a frontier; Isaac took his family beyond it, deeper into turbulent Kansas. They settled about twenty miles beyond Fort Leavenworth, at a place called Salt Creek.

Their troubles were not to come from the Indians or the untamed west. Isaac Cody was a transplanted Northerner, and he had brought his family to a border territory. Kansas was a battleground of opinions. "Slave state or free state" was the controversy. Isaac Cody was a staunch Abolitionist. He tried to keep out of the controversy, but fence-sitting was not his style. One day in Salt Creek he was asked to state his opinion before a crowd of men. Confronted, he stated his position firmly, "I feel Kansas must be a free state, but to keep the peace . . . to avoid friction . . . all Negroes, slaves and free men alike, should be kept out of the territory."

"You black Abolitionist," the crowd yelled, "get the hell out of here . . ."

"I shall always oppose the further spread of slavery," Isaac retorted.

One of the mob jumped forward with knife drawn and stabbed Isaac.

A friend rescued Isaac who had been left by the mob.

From that day on, Isaac Cody was a hunted man. The story of his escape spread and made him a target for any pro-slaver in the territory. Over the next years young Bill would learn to survive in a harsh world. Isaac refused to be forced out. He lived the life of a fugitive. The pro-slavers watched the home in hopes they would catch him if he ever was foolish enough to return. What they didn't know was that he did come back from time to time in various disguises, often as a woman. They also didn't realize that young Will frequently rode to his father's hideouts, having learned to hide his trails.

## A Boy With a Man's Responsibilities...

Mrs. Cody bought a small grocery store which provided them with a meager living, and Isaac had acquired a small sawmill, in another county, under an assumed identity. Even then the family was almost destitute. It was probably because the sawmill did very little business that Isaac was able to keep his real identity secret. Mrs. Cody made just enough to keep a roof over their heads and food in their stomachs. At an early age, Will started to take on odd jobs. During *that time* his mother insisted he attend school to get his formal education. He also became a crack shot, hunting rabbits and birds to provide meat for their table. Before he was ten years old he could shoot a rabbit at a full run, or drop a bird out of the sky in flight—and he wasted no ammunition doing it.

In April of 1857 Isaac returned home sick and exhausted. His family hid him, trying to nurse him back to health, but it was to no avail. The ordeal had destroyed his will, and after a short time, he died. After his father's death, Will stopped attending school. He was now the man of the household. All that he had learned in those three years would serve him well in the future.

A handsome youth. He became bread winner for the family at age eleven — rode Pony Express at age fourteen.

A rare photo of William in uniform for the North during the Civil War.

William had turned eleven when his father died. He became the principal breadwinner for the family. Fortunately he was a sturdy boy, tall for his age. He had sandy brown hair, steady brown eyes, and a charisma that gave everyone a confidence in him. He stood straight and lean with a pride no one would challenge. A handsome boy, he looked several years older than eleven. From early youth he was an individualist and self-confident. Even as a boy he was not to be intimidated. His mother's gentleness and humor came through in him. For all his hardships he was not one to sulk in self-pity.

At Fort Leavenworth he was constantly exposed to dashing cavalrymen, scouts, Indians and Indian chiefs that easterners only read about. He was fascinated by mountain men who came to trade their furs. The stories of wagonmasters ignited his desire to venture west. The horror stories of massacres, lawlessness, and the cruelties of nature further aroused his interest, challenged him. It seemed the entire world was moving westward. Kansas was a major staging area for the migrating pioneers. They weren't just easterners but adventurers from all of Europe and virtually from all the world. He hankered to join this westward tide; to venture out across the Great Plains, past the bison herds, over the majestic Rocky Mountains, and perhaps all the way to the Pacific Ocean.

As more people settled in the west, freight companies sprung up to carry everything from the mail to church organs to the distant frontier settlements. Russell, Majors & Waddell was one of these fast growing freight companies stationed in Fort Leavenworth. Here young Will made the acquaintance of one of its principals, Alexander Majors. His company's huge Conestoga wagons could carry seven thousand pounds of merchandise. Every wagon was drawn by twelve oxen, and each train was made up of twenty to thirty such wagons. The company had contracts with the government and shipped over 16 million pounds of goods in a year, mostly between April and October when the weather was cooperative. To accomplish this feat, the firm required 3500 wagons, 4000 employees, 1000 mules and 40,000 oxen.

Will pleaded with his mother to let him go along on one of the wagon trains as an employee, until she finally consented, but only if he promised to go to school in the fall and winter.

# Will Starts His Career

It was a hard bargain, but Will agreed. His mother went with him to see Mr. Majors to give the needed consent. Majors already knew that Will could ride a horse as well as any adult, and could shoot better than most. The boy was signed on.

His first trip was to New Mexico. They left in early spring. Will's job was to ride messages from one part of the train to another. A caravan that size often strung out over a four to five mile chain from end to end. They also herded along thirty to forty extra head of oxen as spares for those that went lame along the way. There were between 300 and 400 head of livestock to be cared for on each of these trains. At night the trains would "circle up". This created a huge pen for the livestock to graze within.

They could average between twelve to fifteen miles a day and twenty miles on a very good day. The outriders and messengers as scouts would ride several more miles ahead. For Will the work that the oldtimers found a drudgery and a bore was a dream come true. He was the youngest member of the train and the men took a liking to him. He shirked no responsibility, insisted on doing all his work and delighted in helping others when he could. He learned quickly, asking questions about everything and the men enjoyed showing him anything he wanted to know. Before the train was a week out of Fort Leavenworth, he was more than pulling his own weight. His pay was forty dollars a month and food. His salary was paid to his mother.

# Bill's First Moon Shot

Young Will received his first notoriety when bored; he impulsively drew his rifle and took a shot at the moon. When the alarmed encampment came running, weapons in hand, he realized the foolishness of his actions. "I'm sorry. I just shot the moon, pretending it was an Indian."

Will took some good-natured kidding about it from then on, and the story grew. By the time it reached the Leavenworth newspaper, it had changed considerably, and the published version presented Will as, ". . . the youngest Indian slayer of the plains." When he tried to tell people the truth of the matter, they preferred to believe he was being modest. They wanted a young hero in their midst.

Little else was eventful about that first trip, and when he got back home, he wanted to make one more journey before the school term. Mr. Majors sent him to a tough character, Lew Simpson, who was to be wagonmaster of a train headed to Salt Lake. This was part of the famous Colonel Albert Johnston's expedition charged with subduing the rebellious Mormons in Utah.

This trip turned out to be much more eventful than his first. The Mormons had nothing to do with the Federal Government and since the wagon train was under the military, it was attacked by a large Mormon force known as the Danites. This warring group, calling themselves the 'Destroying Angels' were responsible for more than one wagon train massacre.

Lew Simpson was a tough man, but he was no fool. He valued the lives of his men over the goods he carried. Not a shot was fired, except in warning. He and his men were allowed one wagon to carry food and blankets for their return trip. Will walked most of the thousand miles home. "I learned the value of thick soled boots," he always said after that adventure.

It was also during this adventure that Bill first met the famous mountain man, Jim Bridger. He was tough and could survive in the wilderness with nothing more than his knife. If he lost that, there were those who would bet he'd still champion the elements. He never forgot even the smallest detail of any area he'd ever passed through, and he had an uncanny sense of what lay around the next bend or over the next mountain.

Will kept his end of the bargain with his mother and returned to school that fall but when spring came, he was on his way again. Simpson hired him as a general utility man and relief driver, or bull-wacker.

There had been a long-raging argument among wagon masters as to whether mules could pull the heavy wagons faster than oxen. Simpson, a staunch supporter of oxen arranged a race to Fort Laramie for this trip. Though most animals could only do fifteen miles a day with heavily loaded wagons, he intended to get twenty-five miles a day from his oxen. In addition, he selected Conestoga wagons that were constructed tight as ships. Each day his animals put more and more miles between his train and the muledrawn wagons. When his teams reached the Platte River, there was no such thing as a bridge on the Overland Trail. But the muddy banks and the swollen river were hardly an obstacle to them. Where the mules mired down in the ooze, his oxen plodded through, fording the river, pulling the buoyant wagons behind them.

Fort Laramie was nearly a hundred miles northeast of where Laramie, Wyoming now stands. It was at that fort that *Bill,* as they now called him, met Kit Carson. That was the summer of 1858 when Bill was a very impressionable twelve year old. He idolized Carson. He represented everything Bill dreamed of for himself. Kit Carson was already fifty at the time. His reputation as a guide and scout had been legend for decades. He so impressed Bill that years later, he would name his only son after him.

## Bill Befriends The Indians

Fort Laramie was a place where Indians came to trade, and Bill was right there pow-wowing among them. He learned to respect the Indians as a wise people living in harmony with nature and struggling to survive against the *foreigners* from the east. That summer, the Indians Bill befriended at Fort Laramie would save his life in later years. He also learned much of the Indian's sign language, and gained an acquaintance with the speech of the Sioux. That was the summer Bill decided he would be a scout and the West would be his life.

He tried to return to school that fall but the call of the frontier was too strong now. His mother agreed to let him try his hand at fur trapping. Bill and a friend, Dave Harrington, started out with a wagon and yoke of oxen, borrowed from his employers. With meager supplies, traps and some poison for the wolves, they located on Prairie Creek, about two hundred miles west of home. They built themselves a dugout in a hillside which they roofed over with branches and grass thatch. A crude earthen fireplace served to heat and cook on. The endeavor was a disaster!

No sooner had they settled down to business when a bear attacked their camp and killed the oxen. Bill broke his leg, and Dave had to walk back to civilization to get help. While he was gone, Indians looted the camp, leaving Bill with just enough food to keep from starving. "The only reason they spared me was because one of them recognized me from Fort Laramie and had liked me," Bill told his rescuers, weeks later. The boys profited not in furs, but with a lesson in survival.

## Bill Is The Youngest Express Rider

In 1859, Russell, Majors & Waddell was given a government contract to set up a Pony Express route. On April 3, 1860, the first dispatches were sent. Until then the fastest message between New York and San Francisco had been twenty-one days. Express riders cut that down to ten days. The feat required 500 horses, 190 way-stations, 80 riders, and $100,000 to get started, $30,000 a month to keep it going. The cost to send a message across the 3,000 miles was $5 each half ounce. Needless to say, the messages were kept short and were written on the thinnest of tissue paper.

Each rider averaged just under thirty miles, the distance of three stations. Three ponies were used in relays at full gallop, exhausting for the rider as well as the horses. Not infrequently emergencies arose that required a rider to "go an extra leg or two . . . or three". Only the best riders could even be considered for the jobs. Bill was given a trial, with some hesitation, since he was only fourteen years old now, but he did well and was hired on as a regular.

On one occasion Bill had to ride a double stretch because his relief rider had been killed the night before. At the end of the two extra long sections, he had to turn around and ride back to his home station. He set a record in a grueling total ride of more than 300 miles in 21 hours and 40 minutes. On other occasions he had to outride small bands of Indians who often ambushed the express riders.

It was at that time that Bill first met 'Wild Bill' Hickok, who was then a marshal. Wild Bill Hickok was by far the best man in the west with a gun. He was ten years older than Cody. Billy stood in disbelief when he saw Wild Bill place marks on two telegraph poles, then stand between them and with a gun in each hand simultaneously hipshoot both marks dead center. Wild Bill had been hired to bring in some renegade Indians known for raiding express stations and killing employees. Billy went along as part of the posse.

When they came upon the Indians their band was far greater than had been expected. Hickok's posse, outnumbered four to one, decided that there was no way to take the renegades in daylight. They waited for night to attack.

It was not a pretty sight nor a proud moment. Most of the Indians were shot to death as they tried to escape, while Wild Bill lost none of his own men.

That same year Bill Cody had his first run-in with two bandits when they tried to take his horse. Not expecting much resistance from a fourteen year old, they were less than cautious. Bill surprised them when he suddenly hit one over the head with the butt of a gun, then shot the other.

Bill Cody spent alot of time with Wild Bill Hickok. He was already a sure shot, and Wild Bill helped him polish his skill. Hickok was tall and broad shouldered, thin at the waist. He had piercing blue eyes, long blond hair and a curling mustache. Bill called him, "the virtuoso of the Colt revolver." Bill admired anyone skilled with guns and Hickok had no superiors. They became inseparable companions.

The Pony Express lasted only sixteen months. The telegraph replaced it. Russell, Majors & Waddell lost heavily on their investment, but they soon made their losses back by running a stagecoach line. With the ending of the Pony Express, another chapter of William Frederick Cody's story closed.

In 1861, Kansas was admitted to statehood. She was not a slave state. The Kansas-Missouri border was rampant with guerrilla warfare even before the Civil War broke out. Names like John Brown, James H. Lane, Dr. Charles Jennison and William Quantrill struck terror in the hearts of those who lived in the border areas. Bands of men led by these fanatics raided towns and farms, raping, killing, looting what they needed, and burning everything they had no need of.

In 1861 when he was just fifteen, Cody almost enlisted in the Union Army, but his mother begged him not to and convinced him that the family needed him more for its support. She persuaded him to take a succession of jobs; carrying dispatches between stage stations, riding messages and herding on wagon trains, bullwacking and finally, serving as a scout in western Kansas and to Denver. But in the fall of 1863 he was called home. His mother had fallen seriously ill with tuberculosis. He remained by her side until she died in December of that year.

## Bill Goes To War

After her passing he took one more job on the wagons, to provide his sisters with sufficient funds to survive while he'd be away at war. Just prior to his eighteenth birthday, in February of 1864, he enlisted in the Seventh Kansas Regiment. His enlistment form, which he filled out himself, described him as having brown eyes, brown hair, fair complexion and being five feet and ten inches tall, which indicated he had not yet grown to his full height at the time.

The regimentation of military life was not to Bill's liking. He was a true frontiersman, hungering for the freedom of the wide open plains. His heroes were Carson, Bridger, Hickok, his own father, Isaac Cody, individualists all, and he was now of that breed. Because of his background, he was made an army scout, and that gave him the freedom he yearned for to make his military service tolerable. He also took easily to guerrilla warfare, and eventually he was sent into enemy territory as a spy. He infiltrated as far as two hundred miles south of Memphis, Tennessee, disguised as a farm boy. Discovery would have meant instant death by an execution squad, but he volunteered for one trip after another behind enemy lines. He had numerous encounters in which the skills he'd learned on the frontier enabled him to escape.

Later Cody was transferred to the Ninth Kansas Cavalry when they needed a dispatch rider. He served under General Price and was involved in the bloody battle of Pilot Knob where fifteen hundred Union troops were lost. When he was assigned to hospital duty, that ended combat for William Cody. While on duty in St. Louis, Missouri, he met a beautiful school girl, Louisa Frederici.

Cody's usual Express run was 76 miles per day.

In April of 1865 Bill was honorably discharged after fifteen months of military service. He decided he would go west once more to earn a nestegg for Louisa and himself before their wedding. Returning to Leavenworth, he took a job driving stagecoach. Louisa's patience lasted not quite one year; then she insisted Bill give up his wild life to become her husband. On March 6, 1866, they were wed in a simple ceremony, at eleven in the morning, in the bride's parents' home in St. Louis.

William Cody was a stage coach driver after the war.

Bill caused quite a stir when he arrived for his wedding. In the year he'd been away, he let his hair grow long, western style, and also supported a mustache and goatee. He was dressed in buckskins, so uncivilized by eastern standards. No longer the dashing Union soldier of the year before, he was a rough, robust frontiersman. The shock almost provoked Louisa's father to call off the marriage. Only on Louisa's insistence was the ceremony performed.

## Bill Marries Louisa Frederici

Immediately after the wedding the happy couple boarded the luxury sidewheeler, Morning Star—none too soon for Bill—for the trip to Leavenworth. They were to make their home in Salt Creek.

Unhappily for the newlyweds, their divergent backgrounds caused serious conflicts. While he longed for the freedom of the frontier, she was rigidly conventional in her ideas. He was a rough westerner; she, raised in the city, was a proper French girl, with European and Eastern values. She wished them to settle with a job and establish a home and future; he dreamed only of the wide open spaces exploring the mountains. She grew angry and resentful of the sirens *Nature* and *Wilderness* that beckoned her husband. She resorted to violent fits of temper, disliked and insulted his friends, became moody and cried. To please her, Bill agreed to settle down and entered respectable business as a hotel owner. He still owned the old boarding house his mother had acquired in Salt Creek. He named it "The Golden Rule Hotel." His charisma filled the hotel to capacity, but it also attracted the wrong kind of clientele. He was too wonderful a host, and his lavish treatment of guests made the hotel a financial bust. He never understood the word thrift. "Money is to be enjoyed, not collected like trinkets," he'd say. His flamboyance and her conservative nature created more friction than any love could endure. Like the free buffalo that roamed the western plains, he was not to be domesticated.

But it wasn't all strife between Louisa and Bill and in 1867, she became pregnant. Pregnancy, labor and delivery of a baby on the frontier was hazardous in those days. Bill wanted only the best for his wife and expectant child. Medical facilities in St. Louis were far superior, so Louisa returned to have her baby at the home of her parents.

Louisa Frederic Cody — Will's wife.

With the hotel out of business and Louisa back in St. Louis, Bill happily returned to the open country. He hired out as a scout for the army and worked for such notables as General George Armstrong Custer and later for General Sherman and General Philip Sheridan. He also scouted for the Tenth Cavalry, accompanying a Negro regiment of Indian fighters. Though he loved scouting, he still had a distaste for the military and served only as a civilian employee. It was during this time that he adopted his distinctive dress so that he would not be mistaken for a military man. His clothes were a cross between Indian buckskins and flannel worn by the mountain men.

William Cody as a scout. He never liked wearing a uniform; wanted people to know he was a civilian employed by the military.

Cody dressed in his "dude" clothes.

After his stint as scout, Cody became involved in land speculation with William Rose and founded a new town near Fort Hays, Kansas. The town was Rome, Kansas. The venture was designed to make him a fortune that would take care of his family for life, but the forthcoming railroad was rerouted and this venture failed as his hotel business had done. Instead, Hays, Kansas sprung up and almost overnight the citizens of Rome moved their homes and businesses to the new location. Most of the few people who remained in Rome died in a cholera epidemic later that year. When Louisa and baby, Arta, arrived, only to find their dream fade, they returned to her family. Bill hired out as a buffalo hunter for the Kansas and Pacific Railroad. It was that job that gave him the name he would make world famous—"Buffalo Bill" Cody.

Cody's daughter Orra — 1872-1883

# William Cody Becomes "Buffalo Bill"

William Cody worked for the railroads for seventeen months, supplying them with fresh buffalo meat. In that time he killed over 4,000 of the animals. The feat earned him the title of champion buffalo hunter. There were others who did the same kind of work for the military and the railroads. It took a tremendous amount of meat to feed the troops and hungry railroad crews. Of all the hunters, none could supply as many carcasses as Buffalo Bill. His fame and reputation spread so widely that he was finally challenged by Billy Comstock, another buffalo hunter, who also claimed the title of champion, and the name "Buffalo Bill".

In 1869 Buffalo Bill won a contest by killing 69 buffalo in eight hours. In seventeen months he had harvested 4,280 of the animals for the Kansas-Pacific Railroad.

Word of the contest spread like a prairie wildfire. Special trains brought spectators from all over the country. Even Louisa and the baby came out from St. Louis to see the event.

Millions of buffalo roamed wild on the plains. It was estimated that a person could ride a train across the great plains and in one day see as many as twelve million buffalo in the hundreds of herds passed from dawn to dark. They provided a rich food source that seemed endless.

The day of the contest came. Cody was confident that he'd win and made a huge bet on himself. It wasn't only his own skill that he had faith in, but he was sure he had the best gun for the job and the greatest buffalo horse alive. The gun, named 'Lucretia Borgia', was a breech-loading .50 caliber Springfield rifle. Comstock had a Henry rifle that was faster firing, but it lacked the power of Cody's weapon.

Cody's horse, named Brigham after the Mormon leader, was a gift from a Ute Indian who had trained him to hunt buffalo. "That horse knows more about buffalo than any human," Cody boasted. The horse could run among the stampeeding herds, instinctively knowing how they would turn, and which animal to select for the kill. "All I have to do is shoot, reload, and shoot again at the next buffalo he's already picked for me."

On the day of the contest, the two men rode into the herd with an official scorer riding behind each hunter. Cody took off to the right, Comstock to the left, splitting the herd in two. Brigham, in no time, had his group running in a large circle while Comstock's herd headed across the plains with he and his scorer in pursuit. As Cody's herd ran its arc, Brigham would run next to a buffalo with Bill firing at point blank. As the animal fell dead, he'd reload and fire again at the next animal Brigham had selected. And all the time the horse would keep the herd in its stampeeding circle. Cody's first twelve shots brought down eleven buffalo. At the day's end Comstock had downed 46 bison; Cody had killed 69. But while Cody's buffalo dropped in a wide circle, easy for the butchers to pick up on their wagons, Comstock's were spread out all over the prairie. Bill had won the championship and the name of "Buffalo Bill". And since the event received wide publicity, "Buffalo Bill" Cody gained international fame.

The heads of the animals killed in the contest were presented to the railroad and were mounted and hung in every station throughout the country. That, of course, spread the fame of Cody even more, for the railroad stations were the hub of every community where everyone recognized the symbol of the greatest hunter in the world. Soon every buffalo head that hung in any hotel, restaurant or bar was credited to the skill of Buffalo Bill.

Over the next decade it seemed that everyone wanted to try their hand at hunting the big beasts. It was an unforeseen tragedy. Trains were made up to take hunters out on the great plains; men, women and boys shot into the herds from the windows, leaving thousands upon thousand of carcasses to rot. No one would have believed that these great herds of buffalo that numbered as high as sixty million in 1850 would be threatened with extinction by 1880.

## Bill Returns To Scouting

He served under many famous generals.

While still in his early twenties, Buffalo Bill was employed by the Army as a civilian scout. Soon he was elevated to Chief of Scouts by General Phil Sheridan. The appointment came as a result of a heroic ride through hostile Indian territory as a messenger of important dispatches between several frontier forts and outposts. The exhausting ride covered 350 miles in less than 60 hours.

During the time he was Chief of Scouts, a large portion of his time was spent in pursuit of Chief Tall Bull and his band of Indians known as the "Dog Soldiers". The Cheyenne tribal name was derived from the French word *chien* meaning dog. The Dog Soldiers were perhaps the most vicious of fighters among the Indians. Even when Buffalo Bill picked up their trail, it was difficult to find the renegades because even though traveling with their women and children, they could still manage fifty miles a day and the military regiments couldn't keep up.

In the spring of 1869 Bill took a leave of absence to visit his family but after several weeks returned to continue his pursuit of the band of Dog Soldiers who had stepped up their raids on settlers, wagons, railroad workers and trains, even Army patrols. On occasion his path crossed with that of Wild Bill Hickok, who also was scouting for the military.

On July 1, 1869 General E.A. Carr picked up Tall Bull's trail. He set out with five companies of the Fifth Cavalry in hot pursuit of the Dog Soldiers.

Tall Bull, probably because of his past successes, seemingly became overconfident, contemptuous of the white man. He slowed his pace, took less care covering his trail, almost defying the Army to follow him. For ten days General Carr pursued, Cody and some Pawnee scouts reading the trail. On July 11th, Cody convinced General Carr that the Cheyenne were within striking distance. The previous day the Fifth Cavalry had completed a sixty-five mile push through intense heat. "The Dog Soldiers are camped near Summit Springs. We can be upon them by noon today," Cody assured the General. At noon they reached the Cheyenne encampment. Sure that the Army was several days behind, if not lost from their trail altogether, Tall Bull's warriors were sitting around smoking, talking, laughing, least of all expecting the attack called on them by General Carr. The Cheyenne were overwhelmed.

Tall Bull immediately saw that he was beaten. He put his wife and daughter on his horse, jumped up behind and rode the animal out of the encampment. Finding them a safe hiding place in a nearby gulch, he then returned to the hopeless battle. Fifty-two of his braves lay dead; over a hundred had been captured before they could reach their weapons. A handful of his warriors were still armed and able to fight. Tall Bull rallied them and the battle intensified for the moment. Regrouping his braves, Tall Bull led a final charge at the Cavalry. A sergeant saw Buffalo Bill level his rifle at the proud chief and fire. Tall Bull, mortally wounded, fell from his horse which continued the charge riderless. The sergeant caught the animal and after the battle turned the horse over to Cody. Bill named the animal Tall Bull in honor of the chief who had owned him. Cody always rode the horse bareback as his previous master had done. "He's the fastest horse I've ever ridden," Cody often boasted. "He's faster than the wind and chases the freedom Tall Bull always wanted."

Two months after Tall Bull's death, a golden spike was driven into the tracks of the Union Pacific uniting the East and West. The Indian culture, perhaps the only one in the world that fit in perfectly with the scheme of nature, had succumbed to the white man's "civilization".

## Ned Buntline Finds His Hero

E.Z.C. Judson read the newspaper accounts of the battle of Summit Springs with eagerness. He was a dime-novel writer under the pen name of Ned Buntline. He had a somewhat unsavory reputation, living from hand to mouth, staying afloat by sheer wit and cunning. He was a writer, actor, jailbird, beggar, promoter, heavy drinker, and often made temperance speeches if it offered him a chance to make some money to buy his booze. He was the epitome of opportunism. At the time he was reading the accounts of the Summit Springs battle with Tall Bull, he was down on his luck and saw in the story more than just a news dispatch. He had a keen understanding of public nature and the interest people showed in the opening of the West. "If it's a new hero they want," he said to himself, "I mean to give them one."

He'd run out of material for his fiction so he wasted no time in heading for the wild frontier. He was not looking for Buffalo Bill when he started out that summer of 1869. He was intrigued by reports of Frank and Lute North, brothers who had been given much notoriety in the accounts of the battle. Buntline found the North brothers at Fort McPherson, explaining that he wanted to do a book on them. But they were not at all interested. They pointed at Bill Cody snoozing in the shade under a big Conestoga wagon.

Ned met with Buffalo Bill and was immediately enthralled by him. Through his creative talent, the writer made Buffalo Bill a national hero almost overnight. That first story appeared in the *New York Weekly* in December, 1869, entitled "Buffalo Bill, King of the Border Men". It was just what the public had been waiting for and was followed by many others; figments of Ned Buntline's vivid imagination, loosely based on Cody's adventures.

Ned Buntline was only one factor in Buffalo Bill's eventual worldwide fame. A second was far more legitimate. General Phil Sheridan brought Cody into intimate contact with eastern and European high society. When Sheridan returned East after settling the Indian uprisings, he was a hero. His greatest delight was talking about his adventures in the West and his contacts with Buffalo Bill and Bill's prowess as a hunter and scout. It was at President Grant's summer home in Long Branch, New Jersey that he met Commodore James Gordon Bennett II, heir to the *New York Herald*. Bennett wanted to meet Buffalo Bill and have him conduct a buffalo hunt composed of eastern society.

Late in 1871, arrangements were made with the full cooperation of the Army. A train was made up to take the participants out West, and a camp was established near Fort McPherson. A hospital tent was set up as a messhall. Six wall tents with wooden floors housed the "hunters". Carpeting was placed on the wooden floors and regular beds with comfortable mattresses were supplied. Dinners, cooked by a French chef, were served by waiters in full dress and was eaten off of china brought from New York. When Cody showed up and saw the accommodations at the camp, he said only, "Dude wigwams!"

The dudes stood in awe of the hero they'd been reading about in Ned Buntline's novels. Cody appeared in a white buckskin suit, designed and tailored for him by Louisa herself, with white leather fringes. He cut a dashing figure as he rode into camp on a snow white stallion.

A handsome young man, he had a soft baritone voice. He loved to tell stories of his experiences, which he embellished with a great skill he had learned from Ned Buntline. "Guests" were enchanted by the tales. And if anyone ever doubted any of the tall tales Cody related, he soon forgot his doubts when Cody showed off his skills as a hunter when leading the men to the hunt. When they arrived back home, they boasted of their days on the plains with that great friend of theirs, Buffalo Bill. Now it was they who embellished and Cody became a legend.

Several more "dude hunting parties" were led by Buffalo Bill but the crowning event was the arrival in the United States of the Grand Duke Alexis of Russia. After the purchase of Alaska from Russia in 1867, relations between the two countries was at its peak. Emperor Alexander II sent the Grand Duke on a mission of good will. He was already familiar with the exploits of the western hero. Naturally there was no end to his delight when it was suggested that a hunting party could be arranged.

The royal hunt was of highest diplomatic and military priority. An almost minute-by-minute account of the hunt was described in the press. On January 14, 1872, headlines all over the country announced that "The Grand Duke killed his first buffalo today."

General Sheridan had arranged for the famous Sioux warrior, Spotted Tail, and some of his braves to be present at the hunt. Buffalo Bill later admitted that he was very uneasy and doubted the wisdom of permitting the Indians to carry loaded rifles during the hunt. "I was pretty sure Spotted Tail would be a man of honor," he said, "but I wondered if some of his braves might not take advantage of the situation to take revenge on the paleface."

So successful was the hunt that General Sheridan offered Buffalo Bill a commission in the Army; but Cody refused. Meanwhile Bill's name spread from the newspapers and Buntline's dime novels and appeared on theater marquees as his adventures were adapted for the stage.

# THE RAY

VOL. 2.     BOSTON, WEDNESDAY, MARCH 5, 1873.     No. 152.

---

**MORRIS & IRELAND,**

64 SUDBURY STREET,

BOSTON,

## SAFES

Patent Inside Bolt Work.

More secure from Burglars, and no expense repairing Bolts or Locks.

**Champion Record**

IN THE

**GREAT BOSTON FIRE!**

**Morris & Ireland**

Are the ONLY parties who have published a complete record of all the safes they had in the

**Great Boston Fire,**

Including their losses, giving the names of the owners.

They have a record far better than any other Safe, and challenge other manufacturers to publish a full list of their Safes, with names of the owners.

**MORRIS & IRELAND,**

64 Sudbury Street,

BOSTON.

---

## BOSTON THEATRE.

J. B. BOOTH, - - - - - Lessee and Manager.

### The Scouts of the Prairie!

**ENGAGEMENT LIMITED TO SIX NIGHTS AND TWO MATINEES!**

### THIS AFTERNOON,

The Entertainment will commence with a Beautiful Terpsichorean Comedietta, written by Colonel Judson, to introduce the Graceful MORLACCHI in Four Exquisite Dances, entitled

### LOVE'S BATTLE!

Or, Fairy Transformations!

NINETTE, with Entrance Sortita, Spanish Bolera, Caprice Schottice and Polish Mazurka .................................... M'LLE MORLACCHI
CAPT. EUROPE .................................... HARRY WENTWORTH
FIFTEENTH AMENDMENT .................................... GEO. C. DAVENPORT
MADAME DUBOIS .................................... ELLA BEACH

To conclude with Ned Buntline's Sensational Drama of

### SCOUTS OF THE PRAIRIE

BUFFALO BILL (by the original hero) .................................... HON. W. F. CODY
TEXAS JACK (by the original hero) .................................... J. B. OMOHUNDRO
CALE DURG .................................... NED BUNTLINE
MORMON BEN .................................... HARRY WENTWORTH
PHELIM O'LAUGHERTY .................................... GEO. C. DAVENPORT
CARL PRETZEL .................................... WALTER FLETCHER
HAZEL EYE .................................... SENORITA ELOE CARFANO

**INDIANS.**

WOLF SLAYER (specially engaged for this part) .................................... W. J. FLEMING
BIG EAGLE .................................... JOS. J. WINTER
LITTLE BEAR .................................... GEO. B. BEACH
AR-FI-A-KA .................................... GRASSY CHIEF
AS-GE-TES .................................... PRAIRIE DOG
AS-SIN-AN-WA .................................... WATER CHIEF
TE-CO-TIC-POWN .... } Pawnee Indian Chiefs. { .... BIG ELK
KIT-KOT-TONS .................................... GREAT RIVER
CHUK-KAK .................................... SEVEN STARS
DOVE EYE .................................... M'LLE MORLACCHI
NATOLAH .................................... Mrs. BEACH

☞ *For Synopsis of Scenery and Incidents, see third page.* ☜

**MATINEE ON SATURDAY AT 2 O'CLOCK!**

Friday, Benefit of BUFFALO BILL and TEXAS JACK. Saturday Night, Farewell and Benefit of NED BUNTLINE.

**MONDAY, March 10.**—Engagement of the Fascinating Comedienne and Supreme Favorite, **MAGGIE MITCHELL**, who will appear in her excellent impersonation of *JANE EYRE*. Sale of Seats on Thursday.

Musical Director .................................... Mr. N. Lothian
Treasurer .................................... Mr. John M. Ward
Business Agent .................................... Mr. H. A. M'Glenen

☞ The Pianos used in this Theatre are from the celebrated manufactory of CHICKERING & SONS. The Cabinet Organs from the manufacturers, MASON & HAMLIN.

**OPERA GLASSES TO LET AT THE STAND IN THE FRONT LOBBY.**

### SCALE OF PRICES.

Admission .................................... 75 Cents    Balcony and Orchestra .................................... $1.50
Family Circle (Reserved) .................................... 50 Cents    Parquet Circle .................................... $1.00
Dress Circle (Reserved) .................................... 75 Cents    Orchestra Boxes .................................... $10 each
Gallery .................................... 30 Cents    Proscenium Boxes .... According to Location

Box Office open from 8.30 A. M. till 10 P. M., when seats can be secured six days in advance.

Doors open at 1.30 and 7.15. - - Commences at 2 and 7.45 o'clock.

---

**GENUINE GODDARD BUGGIES**

First ORDER completed, and on exhibition at Repository. Parties in want of a first-class Vehicle will do well to CALL and EXAMINE it, and leave an order, so as to have it finished for Spring.

## CARRIAGES

---

### The Scouts of the Prairie.

**SYNOPSIS OF SCENERY AND INCIDENTS.**

ACT I. — *Scene* 1. — On the plains. Cale Durg, the Trapper. Arrival of Buffalo Bill and Texas Jack. Story of the Hunt. A warning from Dove Eye. Danger. "We'll wipe the red skins out." Off on the trail. The war-whoop.
*Scene* 2. — The Renegade's Camp. Mormon Ben. Phelim O'Laugherty and Pretzel. O'Laugherty's continued drouth. Danger to Hazel Eye.
*Scene* 3. — Hazel Eye's poetic tribute to Cale Durg. Hazel Eye surprised. Cale Durg to the rescue. The Renegade foiled. Wolf Slayer, the treacherous Ute. Cale Durg overpowered. Search for the bottle. Cale Durg's temperance rhapsody.
*Scene* 4. — Doomed to the torture-post. Dove Eye's appeal to the Chief. "Death to the Pale Face." Then burn, ye cursed dogs, burn. The blazing fagots. Dove Eye's knife, the severed bonds. Cale Durg defiant. "We'll fight ye all. Death to the Redskin." Rescue of Cale Durg.

ACT II. — *Scene* 1. — Mormon Ben, Pretzel and Phelim O'Laugherty. O'Laugherty declares he is not a Mormon. The meeting with Indians. What Mormon Ben wanted. What O'Laugherty wanted. Wolf Slayer's disdain of fire water. "It's the curse of the Red Man as well as the White." The departure of the Indians for the war-path. Dove Eye's invocation to the Great Spirit.
*Scene* 2. — Dove Eye and the Hazel Eye, the two friends. Buffalo Bill declares his love. It is reciprocated. Texas Jack arrives and interrupts the meeting. "The Indians are coming." Buffalo Bill and Jack retire to ambush. How Jack ropes them in. "Buffalo Bill." "That's the kind of a man I am." How they scalp them on the plains.
*Scene* 3. — The Shakes. Cale Durg to the rescue. God's Beverage. Love scene between Texas Jack and Hazel Eye.
*Scene* 4. — The search for Hazel Eye, "The cage is here, but the bird has flown." The trail. The search and capture of the Forest Maidens. Dove Eye's contempt for the Renegades. Cale Durg arrives upon the scene. "Fly, fly, your enemies are too many." Cale Durg never runs. The capture and death of Cale Durg. The Dying Curse. The Trapper's Last Shot.

ACT III. — *Scene* 1. — Dove Eye and Hazel Eye, Grief of Cale Durg. Buffalo Bill and Texas Jack. Bill's Oath of Vengeance. "I'll not leave a Red Skin to skim the Prairie." Dove Eye dejected. The White Girl and the Red Maiden's affections. "We'll be sisters." Revenge for the Slain Trapper." Vengeance or Death.
*Scene* 2. — The German Trader. The Loss of the Bottle. Carl Pretzel's Agony.
*Scene* 3. — The Scalp Dance. Eagle and Wolf Slayer. "I come to kill you." The Knife Fight. Death of Wolf Slayer. Dove Eye's glorious revenge.
*Scene* 4. — Carl Pretzel and Mormon Ben on their last legs. No prospect for the fiftieth wife.
*Scene* 5. — Dove Eye's faith in the Manitou. The Indians. Buffalo Bill's red hot reception. "Give it to them, boys." One hundred reds for one Carl Durg. The American Scout triumphant. Great Heavens, the PRAIRIE ON FIRE!

---

HATS CAPS AND FURS, AT REDUCED PRICES, BEE HIVE, 132 WASHINGTON STREET.

When Cody launched his Wild West show he was already a legend as a scout, horseman and sharp-shooter. This was taken at about the time of the Grand Duke Alexis of Russia's great buffalo hunt of 1872.

Shortly after the visit of Grand Duke Alexis, Buffalo Bill finally decided to accept the invitations he'd received from the dude hunters. In winter of 1872 he set out for New York, stopping first in Chicago. He was twenty-six. Taken to Marshall Field's Department Store, he was outfitted from head to toe in the latest eastern fashion. When he saw himself in the mirror, he felt conspicuous. "The hair ain't right," he commented, "I got to get it cut. Ain't proper hanging to the shoulders in such a fine store-bought suit."

General Sheridan vetoed the idea, "You can't cut your hair. You're Buffalo Bill and you've got to look like you . . . like your pictures."

It had never occurred to Cody that he had a public image to live up to, but that lesson was enforced when he reached New York and the "dudes" became outraged at the new suit of clothes. "They don't know how to dress in Chicago," they insisted, and dragged Bill off to Heckscher's Exclusive New York Tailor Shop. This time Bill looked into the mirror and felt like he was Beau Brummel of the plains. The public craved to see him "western" and soon he modified his costume to serve wherever he went. The outfit wasn't eastern or western; it was distinctively Buffalo Bill.

Ned Buntline was in New York at the time and took Cody to Niblo's Garden to see a play. It was a stage adaptation of one of his dime novels entitled "Buffalo Bill". Naturally, during the intermission, Cody was introduced to the astonished crowd. It brought the house down. Of course Ned Buntline had anticipated it all. It was all part of his scheme to convince his hero to go on stage. Before Cody returned to the West, he had done two things, completely captured the hearts of the eastern public and made arrangements to start an acting career.

As an incentive to join the theater, Cody was promised $500 a week pay, four times more than he had ever earned in his life and an enormous amount for those days. He couldn't turn his back on such an income with a wife, a daughter, and now a son, Kit Carson Cody, to support.

## Wins Congressional Medal of Honor

During that summer before Cody went on the stage, two events took place that made him an even greater hero to the nation. He took part in one more scouting expedition for the Army and was wounded in battle. The wound was a minor head injury but he fought with such bravery, he was recommended for the Congressional Medal of Honor. The second event was being elected to the Nebraska legislature. It was a total surprise since he didn't run for office, had never been a resident of the state. He accepted the title of "Honorable" and thereafter signed himself as "Hon. William F. Cody" even though he declined the office. He also turned down, with some reluctance, offers to run for United States Senate and Governorships.

Buffalo Bill, Ned Buntline, and Texas Jack Omohundro as they appeared on stage in 1872-73.

## Bill Goes On Stage

Late fall of 1873 when Cody met Ned Buntline in Chicago for the beginning of his stage career, he had forgotten to bring the Indians. But he had brought another scout with him, Texas Jack. Buntline took Bill and Jack to his hotel room and in less than four hours wrote *Scouts of the Plains*. It was so badly written that when critics found out how long its creation had taken, they commented, "It's amazing it took him that long." To make matters worse it was written just days before the opening. In place of the Indians Cody forgot to bring, Ned hired some locals and dressed them up. He hired Italian-Born Mlle. Morlacchi to play an Indian maiden. The press described her as having " . . . an Italian accent with a weakness for scouts." Not to be left out of this unlikely thespian troop, Ned wrote himself a part, that of scout Cale Durg.

Opening night was a sellout beyond their fondest dreams. They grossed $2,800, more than any of them had ever seen at one time in their lives. For their money, the audience witnessed a spectacle unseen before in all of theatrical history. As the curtain raised, Cody was struck dumb with paralyzing stage fright. His was the opening line of the "play" and the other two actors just stared, waiting for him to start. After a long wait Buntline, not knowing what else to do, asked Cody a question that had nothing to do with the script. It shocked Bill back to reality and he started to ad-lib in reply. "You've been off buffalo hunting with Milligan, haven't you?" was the question. What made Ned ask that specific question at such a critical time was even beyond Buntline, but he couldn't have done better. Bill started talking extemporaneously about the hunt in his folksy way that left the audience delighted. For the next three acts the group improvised a totally new play right there on the stage. It was a theatrical first! It was horrible! But the audience loved it! The critics sat in absolute disbelief. They couldn't think of words adequate to describe the catastrophy; even worse, they couldn't understand the positive response of the audience.

For the next few weeks, wherever they took the show, it was a financial success. But with Ned Buntline's creative bookkeeping, Buffalo Bill only realized a profit of $6,000 and expenses by the end of the season. Buffalo Bill's future was launched. He realized that the Indian wars were a thing of the past. There was no future in scouting. He knew that Ned Buntline had exploited him, but he was also intelligent enough to realize that Ned had taught him how he could exploit himself in the future.

John M. Burke, business manager.

Realizing that Buntline was not the man he could trust, Bill looked for other management. He met John M. Burke, an impresario from a stock company theater and put himself in Burke's able hands. It was a relationship that would last for forty successful years.

Wild Bill Hickok, Texas Jack Omohundro, and Buffalo Bill during the Eastern theater circuit of 1874.

To replace Buntline on stage, they persuaded Wild Bill Hickok to join the troop. It was a short association. Wild Bill was incompatible with city life. He got into one fight after another. He couldn't see making an "ass" of himself playacting when he should be out west doing the things he loved most. He felt like a caged animal and shortly after, Wild Bill left the show.

But under Burke's direction the show was a success. Bill became adept at his work, grew to enjoy it, loved the limelight and made fabulous money. He moved his family, Louisa, Arta, Kit and now another daughter, Orra, to Rochester, New York. For the first time Louisa was happy. She felt at home in the eastern city and enjoyed the first financial security of her married life.

Kit Carson Cody, the Colonel's only son who died at the age of six in 1876.

## Tragedy Strikes

The show continued to improve. It seemed as if nothing could ever go wrong. During a performance in Massachusetts Bill received a wire. Five year old Kit was seriously ill with scarlet fever. He got home just in time for the child he loved so dearly to die in his arms. Little Kit was buried in Mount Hope Cemetery in Rochester on the 24th of April, 1876.

Buffalo Bill partly blamed himself for the child's death, a feeling that Louisa tended to reinforce. She had curled the child's long, soft hair which Bill had disapproved of and had it cut. After the child died, he felt that the short hair caused a chill which brought on the illness. Of course there was no truth to it but in a time when medical knowledge was limited, such beliefs were commonplace. After that he tended to spoil his daughters. Buffalo Bill always loved children, and enjoyed playing with them. He delighted in having children come backstage or to his tent after a show. After Kit's death, he cherished their admiration and company even more.

Bill tried to return to his work after the death of his only son, but his grief was too great. He had to get away and the west was the only place his wounds might heal. It led to the most publicized act of his scouting career, an experience he thought he'd never return to.

The Sioux Indians in the Dakotas, what is now Wyoming and Montana, never submitted to the conditions of the treaties of 1863. A people who had lived in harmony with nature for eons could not bind themselves to reservations and white man's rules. And when the whites broke the treaties, the Sioux rebelled. They looked to their great, all-knowing medicine man, Sitting Bull, for guidance. He led his people against the whites who threatened the Indians with annihilation. An Indian war was inevitable by the greed of the whites and the Army further provoked that war. At first the Indians tried to avoid it, but by the spring of 1876, the die had been cast.

The famous Sitting Bull and Cody in 1885, the year the Sioux medicine chief traveled with the Wild West show.

# The Indian Wars

On March 17th the Army attacked an Indian Village on the Powder River in Montana. The Indians escaped but not before they inflicted severe losses on the Army. The attack was propagandized to make the Indians appear the savage aggressors.

The defeat of the Army was just the first of many. Wherever their paths crossed, the Indians were victorious. Sitting Bull was a great strategist; his war chiefs, skilled tacticians, striking swiftly and then vanishing. Sitting Bull's warriors, especially those under the leadership of Crazy Horse, destroyed the military at every engagement. As the news reached the East, the "savagery" was reported in such a way that the Indians were regarded as animals to be exterminated.

Buffalo Bill was playing to full houses in Wilmington, Delaware when a telegram came asking him to return to the frontier as Chief of Scouts. Still grieving deeply over the recent death of his son, his heart had not been on play acting. The telegram was a heaven-sent message to his bereaved mind.

Buffalo Bill at the Indian Congress in 1901. (Left to right) Rain-In-The-Face, Red Shirt, Crazy Head, Red Cloud, Chief Gall, American Horse, Crow King, and Spotted Tail.

Buffalo Bill with Sioux, Crow and Pawnee scouts in 1875.

Impulsively he ran from the theater and caught the next train West. Four days later he arrived in Cheyenne, Wyoming, still in his stage outfit. Truly the stuff heroes were made of. Within the next few weeks the accounts of events and his actions would give the public all they expected from him.

Cody was reattached to his old outfit, the Fifth Cavalry, led by General Carr. On June 22, 1876, they set out to engage the enemy, Buffalo Bill reading the trail for the Army.

On July 10th, word reached General Carr that the Cheyenne were attempting to join forces with the Sioux under Sitting Bull. The Fifth Cavalry was to cut them off. No one knew that the tribes had already come together. Shortly thereafter an alarming message reached Carr: "Custer and all troops, Seventh Cavalry, killed." The Battle of the Little Big Horn was history.

Within the week the Fifth Cavalry came across a war party led by a brave warrior called Hay-O-Wai, or Yellow Hand. Witnesses said that Yellow Hand singled Cody out for his hand-to-hand battle. Both fired at the same instant, but the Indian's shot missed. Cody's bullet passed through Yellow Hand's leg and into his pony's heart. At the same moment that the warrior's animal fell, Cody's horse stepped into a gopher hole at full gallop. Both rider and horse went down. Cody rolled, but came up holding his rifle and instinctively fired, killing Yellow Hand before the war chief could get off a second shot. He took Yellow Hand's scalp and holding it up, shouted, "First scalp for Custer!"

Reenacting the drama of the Yellow Hand duel. Thereafter Buffalo Bill was promoted as part of the Custer legend. The Plains Indians came to regard him as "the other Pahuska" (meaning "Long-hair").

By the time the story reached the East it varied greatly and therein lies a great tragedy. The newspapers and cheap novels so distorted the deeds of Buffalo Bill's heroism, the truth has been lost in wilder, less believable tales. Thus, much of the real bravery that William F. Cody displayed throughout all of his life has been thrown out with the fiction.

John M. Burke had been following the stories that came back from the "war front" and realized that Buffalo Bill was the great American legend.

## Buffalo Bill Obsessed

Buffalo Bill returned to the East, a hero obsessed. He was tired of 'makin' a fool of himself on the stage, bringing a fictitious frontier to the East. "I want to give eastern folks a real taste of the West—with the real people and animals that was the Wild West." The idea had been smoldering in his mind for years. But his public demanded him, and his financial condition dictated that he return to the stage. John M. Burke inflated Cody's image before the public with a flood of articles, books and reviews. They sold well, as did everything else that had his name on it.

Early in 1882, Nate Salsbury came into Cody's life. He was an actor, producer, director from the Park Theater in Brooklyn. He, too, had an idea for a Wild West Show. Their ideas were very compatible, and Nate Salsbury set out to raise the enormous amount of money needed to start them off.

Nate Salsbury — Wild West business manager.

The cast of the original Wild West of 1883.

At the end of the season Bill moved to North Platte, Nebraska where he had built a comfortable home for his family. He named the ranch Welcome Wigwam. In June of 1882, his neighbors decided to put on a 4th of July shindig called the "Old Glory Blow-Out." He was delighted. It was the opportunity he had been waiting for to try out his ideas. He rounded up cowboys, Indians and bought the old Deadwood Stagecoach. He herded up some buffalo and with these ingredients he put on his first outdoor Wild West Show and the start of the modern day rodeo! It was a sensational success. Right then and there he decided to take the show East. He formed a partnership with Doc Carver, a dentist and crack rifle shot. They set up in fairgrounds or empty lots wherever they could get booked into a town. The outfit had a total lack of discipline. The logistics of moving the troupe from place to place were a nightmare. They were suddenly confronted with a thousand problems that hadn't been anticipated; but in spite of it all, the shows "packed them in and left them yelling for more."

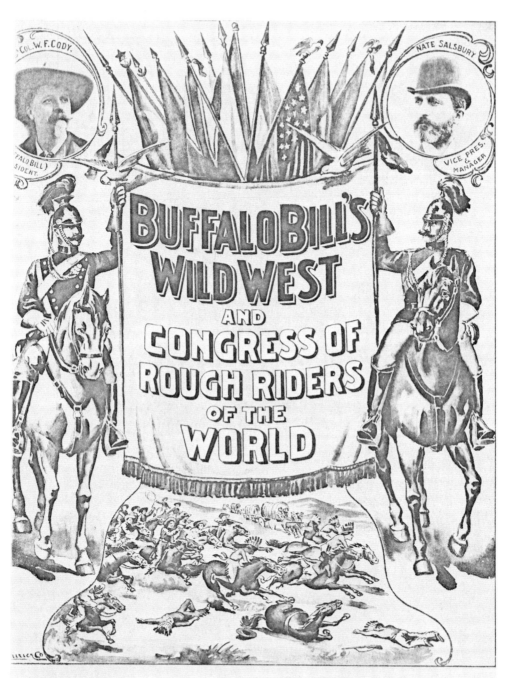

At the end of the season Dr. Carver wanted no more of it. Cody replaced him with a new partner, Nate Salsbury. Nate Salsbury proved to be a better partner than Carver. For days the two labored to work out the details and problems of the show. They got their own train to transport the personnel, stock and tons of equipment. Everyone learned their responsibilities and they did them with precision. That first season they lost only $60,000 but they had things under control. The next tour they grossed millions and by 1901, their net profits reached a million dollars apiece.

On November 24, 1886 the show opened in New York's Madison Square Garden. It was a triumph! In the following ten weeks over a million New Yorkers saw the Wild West!

Col. Cody, a man of distinction and vision; one of the few photos of him in uniform — 1880.

## Cody Hits Europe

In May of 1887, the Buffalo Bill Wild West Show arrived in London, England. Queen Victoria, who was celebrating her fiftieth year on the throne and the people of England took Buffalo Bill and his troupe to their hearts. That same year Cody was made an honorary colonel in the Nebraska National Guard, a title he was most proud of. After that he was referred to as "Colonel".

Part of the Wild West of 1887. They brought frontier America to Europe.

Though the Queen had intended to stay for an hour—the English were surprised that she even appeared at all—she stayed for the entire performance. She was so amazed by the skill and professionalism exhibited, she asked the performers be presented to her in person, an honor reserved for a very special few. That would have been enough to cause a stir throughout the Kingdom, but then she stated she wanted to see the show again and insisted that all the Royal guests of the Fiftieth Jubilee see it too. She arranged a command performance at Windsor Castle. It took place on June 20th. The guests included the Kings of Greece,

When Pope Leo XIII invited the Wild West Company to the Vatican, Cody toyed with the idea of racing the Deadwood stage coach in the Roman Coliseum until he arrived and found it cluttered with stone; he settled, instead, for a photograph of the Buffalo Bill troupe in front of the ancient arena.

The Wild West in France.

Saxony and Denmark, the King and Queen of Belgium, the Crown Prince of Austria, the Prince and Princess of Saxe-Meininger, the Crown Prince of Sweden and Norway, Prince Victor of Prussia, the Duke of Sparta, Grand Duke Michael of Russia, Prince George of Greece, Prince Louis of Baden, and the Prince and Princess of Wales. Cody gave four of the kings a ride in the Deadwood Stage with the Prince of Wales beside him up front. The Prince commented, "You have quite a poker hand there, with four kings in your hand." Cody laughed, but not to be outdone, replied, "It's better than that, I have four kings and a joker prince, that's better than a royal flush."

It was no wonder, that with such a reception by English royalty, every show in England was a sell-out.

The following year the show had a sensational season back in the U.S. In 1889 they went to Europe. To insure its success on the continent, Salsbury decided to open the tour at the Paris Exposition of 1889. Again the shows were sold out, but so were they everywhere else they went, with the exception of Spain. In Spain the weather was bad and the crowds were less enthusiastic because there was no bull fighting. In every country on the continent, the leaders and royalty insisted on riding in the Deadwood Stage during the show. It became a new status symbol.

Cody disliked the term "show". He never applied it to his own creation which he called "Buffalo Bill's Wild West".

Buffalo Bill's Cowboy Band.

# *Buffalo Bill Made a Hit In Europe*

There are whole books devoted to Buffalo Bill's tour of the European continent with his Wild West show. There is apparently no doubt that he made a big hit.

He was painted by a Parisian artist, Rosa Bonheur. He gave a command performance for royalty. He staged a western-style breakfast in a tent, cooked by Indians, for English royalty.

The show went to Paris, London, Rome, Venice and other cities. It is suggested in "Buffalo Bill and the Wild West", by Henry Blackman Sell and Victor Weybright, 1955, that his title of colonel was a help to Cody in Europe, perhaps smoothing the way for him in titled English society.

A book about this period is "Four Years in Europe with Buffalo Bill", by C.E. Griffin, 1908.

The first time the Wild West show made the scene in Europe, in England, is described in detail in a chapter entitled "Before the Crowned Heads of Europe" in a book by Don Russell, "The Lives and Legends of Buffalo Bill".

As to who made the trip, Russell quotes London newspapers with this count: ". . . . 83 saloon passengers, 38 steerage passengers, and 97 Indians, . . . 180 horses, 18 buffalo, 10 mules, 10 elk, 5 wild Texas steers, 4 donkeys and 2 deer."

Annie Oakley, Red Shirt, chief of the Sioux, Old Charlie, Buffalo Bill's horse and various others were included in the company.

In London, especially, the reception for this first Wild West show abroad was tremendous. Queen Victoria had observed mourning for her consort, Prince Albert, for 25 years. Yet she attended the show.

In Italy a request was made that Buffalo Bill's cowboys try to tame some of the country's wildest horses. They were animals that had never been subdued, and the crowds turned out to see the results of the challenge. There was bitter disappointment when it took the cowboys less than five minutes to break the animals. After that they were given the same challenge in every country they visited. Each nation would scour the land for the wildest animals they could find, with the same results. The horses were tamed in just minutes by the American riders.

A rare F.J. Hiscock photo of Buffalo Bill — 1907

## Wild West A Fabulous Success...

Through the years the show grew more spectacular. They kept in the best and added new acts constantly. The troupe grew to over five hundred employees. The show became a national institution and was in constant demand. Life for Buffalo Bill became a series of one-night stands throughout the country that continued for almost twenty years. And even with his active social life and personal demands, Cody rarely ever missed a show. The train ran almost twelve thousand miles in a season of 200 days. There were over 340 performances at 132 locations.

# ...Then A Sad End

The year 1912 was Buffalo Bill's last year with the Wild West Show he had built. He was sixty-six years old. Cody had made a fortune out of the shows while Nate Salsbury managed his financial affairs, but after Nate died in 1902, Cody's fortune dwindled. In that last decade that he performed, creditors began hounding him from all sides. He made poor investments and was an easy mark for unscrupulous or inept partners in dozens of ventures.

Buffalo Bill in his later years — 1915

Sisters of Buffalo Bill; Lidia, Julia, Mary (May), and Helen.

In 1913 Colonel Cody visited his sister in Denver and there met H.H. Tammen who with Fred Bonfils owned the Denver Post. Cody told him that he needed $20,000 to get out of debt. Tammen agreed to lend it to him for six months, taking a note on the show property as collateral. Six months later Tammen seized the show. Frantically Cody tried to raise the money he needed. He went to friends for whom he'd been doing favors for a lifetime. No one seemed to remember the past generosity of the man who was now reduced to begging from them. It was hopeless. A few weeks later everything fell victim to the auctioneer's gavel.

Col. Cody with his wife — taken at Chahalis, Washington two years before his death.

Over the next few years Cody tried to make several comebacks but everything seemed to fail. He even tried to get into motion picture production of the first westerns. Some people feel that it was the motion picture industry that helped destroy Buffalo Bill because it could bring the West to the general public so realistically, and for just the few cents that it cost for a movie ticket.

Finally his health started to fail. He no longer had the strength to mount and ride his horse at public appearances and took to driving a phaeton hitched to a team of white horses. Once again his debtors hounded him. Again Harry Tammen helped him out, but not without it being to his own advantage. Tammen reduced Buffalo Bill to an attraction in his Sells-Floto Circus. It hurt his pride deeply, "I feel like a freak in his side show."

Last photo of Col. Cody taken in Glenwood Springs, Colorado, in December, 1916.

## Cody's Last Performance

Buffalo Bill Cody made his last appearance on November 11, 1916 in Portsmouth, Virginia. He was ill with an upper respiratory infection. He went on despite great pain and every breath was an ordeal. Fear clutched at him, fear of dying before all those people. After the show he set out for home.

Enroute he stopped off in Denver where his sister, May lived. Horrified at his appearance, she tried to convince him to stay and recuperate, but he insisted on going on to his home in Cody, Wyoming. There among friends he recuperated and rapidly gained strength. In December he returned to Denver to try to raise money for a new venture to regain his lost fortunes. The trip was too much for him. He started to develop uremia. On the suggestion of his doctor in Denver, he was sent to Glenwood Springs for the curative spring waters. There he collapsed. He was returned to Denver in hopes he would regain strength enough to return to Cody where he wished to be buried.

When his condition worsened, his wife and daughter came to be with him in Denver. On the morning of January 10, 1917, William Cody asked his doctor, a Dr. East, " . . . answer me honestly. What are my chances?"

"There is a time, Colonel, when every honest physician must commend his patient to a higher power," Dr. East replied.

Solemnly, Bill asked, "How long?"

"Your life is like an hourglass, the sand slipping gradually, slowly . . . the end is not far away."

Cody asked for his brother-in-law, Lew Decker, to play him high five poker. At noon, January 10, 1917, the Hon. Colonel William Frederick "Buffalo Bill" Cody died. He was almost seventy-one years old.

The man who had done so much to destroy Cody in his last years, Harry Tammen, would once more play a part. It had been Cody's wish to be buried in a spot he'd selected years earlier, on Cedar Mountain, overlooking Cody, Wyoming. Tammen took the matter in his own hands and made arrangements to entomb Buffalo Bill in his present gravesite, atop Lookout Mountain, overlooking Golden, Colorado and the vast plains which he loved so much.

Goldie Griffith, former cowgirl and bronc rider with Buffalo Bill's Wild West Show stated in a tape recorded interview on May 23, 1972 at home in Nederland, Colorado, " . . . that place up there (Lookout Mountain), he called it 'Point Lookout,' and it was on a Sunday when he couldn't parade and he said, 'Come on now, I'm going to show you where I'm going to sleep, the most beautiful scene you ever saw!' "

Despite this conclusive eye-witness account, controversy still persists on the issue of where Buffalo Bill wanted to be buried.

Peter Fillerup — "Buffalo Bill the Showman" — 1980 Bronz, donated by the owners of the Buckhorn Exchange Restaurant, where Cody spent a lot of his time prior to his death in 1917.

Although he had killed several Indians, he had never shot a white man, so the term "killer" was never applied to him. Cody often guided hunting parties for famous visitors including Duke Alexis, son of Russian Czar Alexander II. Newspapers all over the country followed the visit and reports of Cody's skill as guide and hunter spread his fame.

His partnership with Buntline ended after one season but Cody continued a pattern for the next ten years. In summer, he scouted for the army and guided hunting parties. In fall, he resumed touring with his Buffalo Bill Combination, the theatrical troupe that was the forerunner of the western extravaganza he later developed.

Colonel Cody, well named America's foremost American, who has been honored wherever he has been received, and though past three score and ten still is acknowledged as the greatest drawing card in the world, year in, year out.

Col. W.F. Cody in Rome, Italy, 1887, a peak in his career.

"Buffalo Bill" gained his nickname in 1867-68 when he provided buffalo meat for construction crews on the Kansas Pacific Railway. He claimed to have killed 4,280 buffaloes in 17 months.

Cody popularized the now familiar Stetson cowboy hat as well as the Imperial mustache and beard.

Cody managed and starred in his *Wild West* for thirty years, from 1883 to 1913.

Cody's flare for mixing theatrics and real life led him quite naturally to the creation of *Buffalo Bill's Wild West*.

Buffalo Bill in 1915 with his carriage. He gave up his saddle for a buggy seat.

Thousands of letters went out to Boy Scouts, Campfire Girls and anyone who wrote to him. Cody frequently had visitors at his tent at the show grounds. His English valet kept a large glass filled with "Old Yellowstone" on the desk. Every few minutes Bill would gulp a few swallows, but he was never drunk. He wrote letters to the early hours of the morning, and during the day when he could find time. He answered the thousands of letters that came to him, especially enjoying those from kids.

The decline of the *Wild West* was partly a mark of its success. Once the cowboy was respectable and the Indian made as attractive as repulsive, a large part of the thrill of seeing them in action was lost.

An interesting note for military personnel is that the Congressional Medal of Honor was conferred on Cody for valor in fighting Indians on the Platte River in 1872. However, the medal was rescinded in 1917 because he was not a member of the Armed Forces at the time of his feat.

A superb horseman all his life, Cody rides Isham to inspect the show grounds.

Cody's favorite photo, showing his famous saddle, lariat and gun.

The show consisted of such famous people as Sitting Bull (of Custer fame), Annie Oakley, Johnny Baker, and Indians, Cavalry, Cowboys and Gauchos.

Cody was an easy mark for con artists. He invested over a hundred-thousand dollars in an Arizona gold mine and lost it all. Mines always intrigued him. He even invested in some that never existed.

Home-spun natives back West feted him with the title "Honorable" by electing him to the Nebraska State Legislature in 1872; the Governor appointed him "Colonel" in the National Guard some time later. He made good use of the title to legitimatize and elevate his *Wild West* entertainment: he was always introduced as "the Honorable William F. Cody" or "Colonel Cody."

A dinner for Nate Salsbury (white beard). Guests include: Iron Tail, Johnny Baker and Cody.

Arta Cody — daughter — 1866 - 1905.

Irma Cody — daughter — 1883 - 1918.

A World Champion Bronc Rider

Goldie Griffith Cameron was one of the five women bronc riders who traveled with the Wild West. Farmers and ranchers always brought in wild horses they wanted saddle-broken. "Often they'd bet we couldn't ride 'em. Us lady bronc busters would take their bets, and usually their money." Girls in the show were not allowed to wear trousers, and had to create special skirts and bloomers. "Cody was a good man who we all loved and respected," Goldie said of Buffalo Bill. "He'd give you a nickle of his last dime. He wouldn't tolerate anyone who was a trouble maker. We were like one big happy family . . . we were all very close."

Part of the special Goldie Griffith exhibit.

Goldie Griffith was a whiz as a bronc rider. She could break the most difficult of broncs. And she was beautiful as well. Her friends said of her, "She's as smooth as a new born calf, and a barrel of fun." She was a born prankster. Her husband, Bernie St. Clair, was also a bronc rider with the Wild West, but not nearly as skilled as Goldie.

When he started with the Wild West, Johnny Baker was billed as "The Cowboy Kid."

Johnny Baker was a crack shot, coached by both Annie Oakley and Cody.

Johnny Baker — "The Cowboy Kid"

Lewis H. "Johnny" Baker was born near North Platte, Nebraska, in 1869, the town which Buffalo Bill called home after 1870. Buffalo Bill's son, Kit Carson Cody, died of scarlet fever in the spring of 1876. Buffalo Bill, who had been Johnny's hero, came to think of Johnny Baker as his own son. They were inseparable. When the Buffalo Bill Wild West Show made its first tour in 1883, Johnny Baker, then 13, went along. He stayed with the show until it closed thirty years later, probably the only person to stay with the show through its entire history except for Buffalo Bill himself. Johnny was featured as "The Cowboy Kid". He was coached in marksmanship by both Cody and Annie Oakley. Shooting contests with Annie became an exciting part of the show, but he never quite became her equal in marksmanship, though his skills were fantastic. He was also an expert rider and roper. As he grew older he took on many of the responsibilities of management of the show. He became Arena Director. He and Buffalo Bill were devoted to each other. In a letter to Johnny Baker, Buffalo Bill wrote: " . . . For twenty-three years you have never once failed me. No father ever had a son more loving and faithful. You have done as much to make Buffalo Bill's Wild West what it is as I have myself . . ."

After Buffalo Bill's death, Johnny Baker tried unsuccessfully to revive the Wild West show with Cody's wife. He then retired with his own wife, Olive, to Estes Park, Colorado, where they operated a restaurant. It was then that they conceived the idea of this museum. The building was begun in 1920, with the cooperation of the City of Denver. Under the direction of Johnny Baker the museum flourished.

On April 24, 1931 Johnny Baker died at Denver's Mercy Hospital, after an extended illness. His wife, Olive, managed the museum until her death in 1956. The world owes Johnny Baker a debt of gratitude for having preserved many of the items which make up the Buffalo Bill Memorial Museum collection.

Johnny Baker and his wife Olive. After his death, she continued to manage and run the Buffalo Bill Memorial Museum. Together they were responsible for preservation of many of the exhibits.

Johnny Baker — founder of the Buffalo Bill Memorial Museum.

Johnny was more than a trick shot. As he grew older he was given more responsibility. He became one of the world's finest arena managers, keeping the show going on schedule. He was with the Wild West for its entire 30 year existence.

Train wrecks were among the major perils of outdoor shows. One of the least publicized of those suffered by Buffalo Bill's Wild West occurred April 7, 1904, on the Chicago & North Western Railway a mile west of Melrose Park, Illinois. When the Wild West train had a head on collision, Annie Oakley was seriously injured, and had to leave the show. Many of the animals died or had to be put to sleep.

Annie Oakley — Little Sure Shot — was born on August 13, 1860, in Darke County, Ohio, to Susan and Jacob Moses. Her real name was Phoebe Ann Moses, but all her friends called her Annie. The family was Quaker. Her father died when she was only five, and her mother was left to care for the seven children.

When Annie was just eight she learned to use her father's old rifle with such skill that she provided the table with meat and had ample game left over to sell to neighbors. She actually paid off the mortgage on the family home with her hunting skill.

Her marksmanship was boasted around the county, and she was frequently entered into shooting matches. It was at one of these shooting matches in 1875 that she met the champion marksman, Frank Butler. They were married a year later. She joined her husband's shooting act under the name 'Annie Oakley.'

In 1880 they joined the Four-Paw and Sells Brothers Circus. There she became an expert rider, and did some of her most difficult shots from horseback. In 1882, she met the great Chief Sitting Bull, who was so impressed with her that he adopted her to his tribe, and gave her the nick-name "Little Sure Shot."

In March of 1884 Annie and Frank joined the Buffalo Bill Wild West Show, and continued to travel with it for seventeen years. In 1901, Annie was seriously injured when the Buffalo Bill Wild West train was involved in a head-on collision. It forced her to leave the show. After having surgery and recuperating, she restricted her activities to exhibitions and some stage appearances. After an auto accident in 1921, she spent months in a hospital, and never again could walk without a brace. She and Frank retired in Ohio, near her birthplace, family and friends. She died on November 3, 1926, and Frank just 18 days later. On Thanksgiving Day of that year, their ashes were interred in Brock Cemetary, near the place of her birth. The Garst Museum in Greenville, Ohio, houses a fine collection of her momentos.

Annie Oakley, "Little Sure Shot," was a champion shot and long-time favorite in the Wild West Show.

Annie Oakley was treated like a lady, despite the unlady-like nature of her profession; the performers were all "champions," "first-rate," or "first-class," and treated with due respect.

Sitting Bull adopted Annie Oakley as his daughter, naming her "Little Sure Shot."

Annie Oakley about 1890.

A Curtis original . . . one of the many rare Indian photographs owned by the museum.

Geronimo — most feared of all Apache warriors. His name struck terror in the hearts of even the bravest Indian fighters . . . until he joined the Wild West.

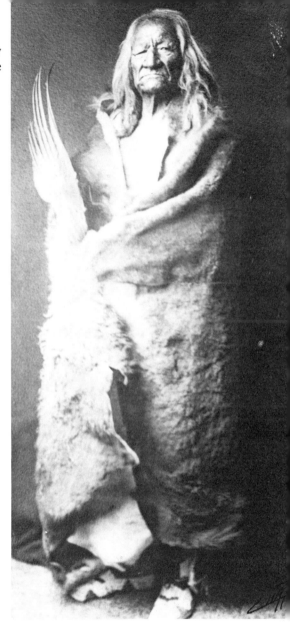

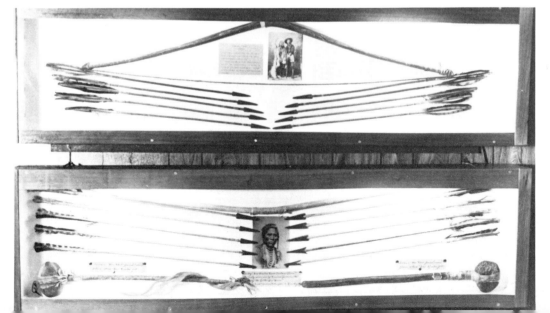

He was with the Cody show for 20 years, and also spent some years with the 101 Ranch Wild West and other circuses. He toured Europe with Cody. In 1904 Cody took Iron Tail along on a hunting trip near Cody's old TE ranch in Wyoming.

Iron Tail, the Indian who modeled for the Buffalo Nickel, and Lone Bear, another Sioux, were both important members of the Wild West.

Iron Tail was an excellent model because he had so many of the characteristics attributed to the American Indians. He looked of dignity, stately bearing, pride, and had an imposing presence.

The cast of the 1912 Wild West Show.

# Buffalo Bill's Wild West

COL. W.F. CODY, *President.*
NATE SALSBURY, *Vice-President.*
MAJOR J.M. BURKE, *Gen'l Manager.*

### DIRECTORS OF TOUR.
JAS A. BAILEY,      W.W. COLE.
LOUIS E. COOKE, *General Agent.*

### BUSINESS MANAGERS.
For Cody & Salsbury,    For Bailey & Cole,
JULE KEEN.           ERNEST COOKE.

### SECRETARIES.
For Cody & Salsbury,    For Bailey & Cole,
L.E. DECKER,          JOS. F. QUAID.

### TREASURERS.
For Cody & Salsbury,    For Bailey & Cole,
JULE KEEN.         FRED B. HUTCHISON.

### DIRECTOR OF ENTERTAINMENT.
JOHN BAKER.

### SUPERINTENDENT OF GROUNDS.
HENRY BARNUM.

### MANAGERS OF PRIVILEGES.
Messrs. DREW AND CAMPBELL.

### GENERAL STAFF.
John Baker, . . . . . . . . . . . . . . . *Arenic Director.*
John McLaughlin, . . *Master of Transportation.*
Dan Taylor, . . . . . . . . . . . . . . *Master Mechanic.*
M.B. Bailey, . . . . . . . . . *Sup't of Electric Lights.*
Jake Platt, . . . . . . . . . . . . . . . *Sup't of Canvas.*
Chas. Evans, . . . . . . . . . *Sup't of Baggage Stock.*
W.W. Reedy, . . . . . . . . . *Sup't of Bronco Stock.*
C.W. Ramsey, . . *Sup't of Confectionery Dep't.*
Wm. Sweeney, . . . . . . . . . . . . *Leader of Band.*
Wm. McCune, . . . . . . . . . . *Officer of the Day*
Morris Kern, . . . . . . . . . *Principal Door Tender*
J.W. Rogers, . . . . . . . . . . . . . . . . . . *Detective*
J.J. McCarthy, . . . . . . . . . . . . . . . . . . . *Orator*
Lou. Decker, . . . . . . . . . . . . . . . *Mail Carrier*
John Noble, . . . . . . . . . . . . . *Head Car Porter*
Keen & Langan, . . . . . . . . . . . . . . . . *Caterers*
M. Martin, . . . . . . . . . . . . . . . . . *Head Waiter*
John Stacks, . . . . . . . . . . . . . *Parade Wardrobe*
Chas. Wichelhausen, . . . . . . . . . . . . *Properties*
Wm. Smith, . . . . . . . . . . . . . . . . *Ammunition*

### DEPARTMENT OF PUBLICITY.
Louis E. Cooke, . . . . *General Advance Manager*
M. Coyle, . . . . . . . . . . . . . . *Railway Contractor*
Edward Arlington, . . . . . . . . . . *Excursion Agent*
Major John M. Burke, . . . . *General Press Agent*
Frank J. O'Donnell, . . *Contracting Press Agent*
Miss Maymie Jester, . . . . . . *Special Press Agent*
Dexter E. Fellows, . . . . . . . *Special Press Agent*
S.H. Semon, . . . . . . *General Contracting Agent*
E.H. Woods, . . . . . *Assistant Contracting Agent*
M. Manton,
Chas. Curtis,     . . . . . . . . . . . . . . *Bill Inspectors.*

### ADVERTISING CAR NO. I.
P.S. Mattox, *Manager.*
W.H. Alberts, . . . . . . . . . . . . *Boss Bill Poster*
Tom Lyons, . . . . . . . . . . . . *Boss Lithographer*
Chas. Hayes, . . . . . . . . . . . . . . . . . *Secretary*
John Lewis, . . . . . . . . . . . . . . . . *Programmer*

### BILL POSTERS
Lew Curry,       Richard Le Fever,
Oliver Lester,      Chas. Welsh,
Geo. Baldwin,      Martin Slivers,
Harry Campbell,    John Alvather,
Pete Dunn,         Sam Sanders,
R.L. Bean, *Car Porter.*

### LITHOGRAPHERS
Fred Seyboth,             John Gray,
Chas. R. Coleman.

### ADVERTISING CAR NO. 2 — EXCURSION DEPARTMENT.
Al. Riel, *Manager.*
Geo. Frazier, . . . . . . . . . . . . . *Boss Bill Poster*
Kurt Eisfeldt, . . . . . . . . . . . . . . . . . *Lithographer*
Chas. Venable, . . . . . . . . . . . . . . . *Banner Man*
Al. Boshell, . . . . . . . . . . . . . . . . . . *Board Man*
Victor Cooke, . . . . . . . . . . . . . . . . . *Card Man*

### EXCURSION BILL POSTERS.
Thos. Deansfield,     H. Sayers,
Wm. Shea,            Chas. Dering,
A.J. Choffin,          Wm. Fannon,
Geo. Houghtaling,    Geo. Nelson,
Dan Pheney,          H. Robinson,
H. Leschinsky,       Chas. Loughridge,
Geo. Hurst, *Car Porter.*

### OPPOSITION BRIGADE
Fred Beckman, *Manager.*
Dan Pheney, . . . . . . . . . . . . . *Boss Bill Poster*
Kurt Eisfeldt, . . . . . . . . . . . . . . . . . *Lithographer*
Herman Leschinsky,
Frank Raymond,    . . . . . . . . . . . . *Bill Posters*

### LAYERS-OUT.
Harry G. Barnum,        Thos. Clear.

### TICKET SELLERS.
### MAIN TICKET WAGON
Fred B. Hutchison,        John Flandreau.

### OUTSIDE TICKETS.
John Tippetts,           Lou. Decker,
Frank Cloud.

### DOWN-TOWN OFFICE
Harry Gray.

### DOWN-TOWN ORATOR.
S.H. Davis.

### RESERVED-SEAT TICKETS.
Jule Keen *in charge.*
Starr Pixley,             Geo. Dittmar,
Sam. T. Bitmead.

### MAIN DOOR TENDERS.
J.P. Brogan,          Dan. Taylor,
Morris Kern,       John McLaughlin.

### RESERVED-SEAT TENDERS.
Walter H. Cleary,      Arthur Waterman.

### USHERS.
Wm. McCune, *Head Usher.*
Dave Jarrett, *Assistant.*
Eddie Walton, *Assistant.*

### RESERVED-SEAT USHERS.
Ed. Barry,           Wm. Hunter,
M. Quinlan,         Ed. Howard,
Geo. Davis,         Wm. Hutton,
Ed. Gallagher,      Sam. Maitland,
Wm. King.

### BLUE SEATS.
Wm. Arnold,        Lee Fuller,
Mike Burns,         Wm. Murphy,
Larry Eagan,       T. McBurney,
Fred Gibson,       G. Pratt,
Geo. Smith,         J. White.
John Condon, *Director.*
Jos. Collins, *Wardrobe.*

### COWBOY BAND.
Wm. Sweeney, *Leader.*
Wm. Sweeney, . . . . . . . . . . . . . . . . *Solo Cornet*
Albert Ziehm, . . . . . . . . . . . . . . . . *Solo Cornet*
Floyd O'Hara, . . . . . . . . . . . . . . . *Solo Cornet*
Jas. Allen, . . . . . . . . . . . . . . . . . . *First Cornet*
W.N. Tinkham, . . . . . . . . . . . *Second Cornet*
Elmer Parlett, . . . . . . . . . . . . . . . . . . *Eb Cornet*
Harry Nelson, . . . . . . . . . . *Solo Bb Clarinet*
Christian Schetting, . . . . . . . *Solo Bb Clarinet*
Frank Genter, . . . . . . . . . . . . . *First Clarinet*
Harvey Benham, . . . . . . . . . . *Second Clarinet*
Frank Carothers, . . . . . . . . . . . . *Eb Clarinet*
Chester C. Larned, . . . . . . . . . . . . . . *Piccolo*
Ed. Weber, . . . . . . . . . . . . . . . . . . *First Alto.*
John C. Howard, . . . . . . . . . . . . *Second Alto*
W.H. Dickin, . . . . . . . . . . . . . . . . . *Third Alto*
John Galligan, . . . . . . . . . . . . . *First Trombone*
Lon Williams, . . . . . . . . . . . *Second Trombone*
Chas. Baas, . . . . . . . . . . . . . . *Third Trombone*
Thos. V. Murphy, . . . . . . . . . . *First Baritone*
John Schilling, . . . . . . . . . . . *Second Baritone*
W.A. Frank, . . . . . . . . . . . . . . . . . . . . . . . *Bass*
M.A. McAdams, . . . . . . . . . . . . . . . . . . *Bass*
Geo. C. Foehlinger, . . . . . . . . . . *Small Drum*
Geo. W. Turner, . . . . . . . . . . . . . . *Bass Drum*

Johnnie Baker, *Expert Marksman.*
Miss Annie Oakley, *Lady Rifle Shot.*
Frank Butler, *Manager for Miss Oakley.*

### DRIVER OF STAGE COACH.
John F. Burke.

### U.S. CAVALRY.
Jas G. Warren, *Sergeant.*
Chas. Reith, *Color Bearer.*

Wm. Baker,          Frank Stryker,
J. Wortman,         W.J. Taylor,
Dennis Langan,     Chas. Humberstone,
Peter Fay,           Ed. Gallagher,
Harry Jackson,      Jas. Brown,
Granville Corr,      Andy Milen,
Frank McCormack.

## U.S. ARTILLERY.
Herman Kanstein, *Sergeant.*

**PIECE NO. 1.** *Drivers*
J. R. Myerly,
Thos. Gibney,
Chas. Wolff,
Jack Langan, *Corp.*
L. Wagner, No. 1.
R. Hegeman, No. 2.
C. Hobart, No. 3.
Jas. Degnen, No. 4.

**PIECE NO. 2.** *Drivers*
Harry Wilkes,
R.I. Clapham,
Jas. Ryan,
Victor Hudson, *Corp.*
C. Triangel, No. 1.
Pony Moore, No. 2
A. Miller, No. 3.
Geo. Davis, No. 4.

## ROOSEVELT'S ROUGH RIDERS.
G.A. Webb, *Sergeant.*
Wm. McGinty, *Color Bearer.*

M.L. Newcomb,
F. Beal,
T. Holmes,
W. Cook,
Tom Isbell,
V.D. Miller,
Jess Langdon,

J. Kline,
Ed. Loughmiller,
F. Bryne,
Ben Miller,
H. Meagher,
J.H. Tait,
L. Muxlow.

## AMERICAN COWBOYS.
Joe Esquivel, *Chief.*
John Franz, *Assistant.*

Silas Compton,
Bert Schenck,
Jim Gabriel,
Jas. Jennings,
Walter Scott,
Jack Joyce,

Jesse Nelson,
Tom Hunter,
Bob Singletree,
Lem Hunter,
Carl Sorrensen,
A. McCann.

## ENGLISH LANCERS.
Thos. Cook, *Sergeant.*
W. House, *Color Bearer.*

Fred Rapley,
J. Clark,
Jas. Ryan,
Wm. Wandland,
P. Shingler,
T. Pigott,

E. Plummer,
W. Ridgwell,
W. Barrett,
T. Dennis,
A. Brown,
W. Pocock.

## GERMAN CUIRASSIERS.
Julius von Natzmer, *Captain.*
Heinrich Sprittule, *Sergeant.*
O. Weinrich, *Color Bearer.*

E. Wittmann,
C. Shultz,
G. Kaempfer,

T. Schwark,
H. Damm,
A. Zippliss,
A. Rother.

## MEXICANS.
Vicente Orapeza, *Chief.*

Manuel Pena,
Epifania Martinez,
Luio Alba,
Santiago Munoz,

Pedro Aleman,
Yrineo Munoz,
Manuel Castillo,
Agapita Alba.

## COSSACKS.
David Cadjaia, *Chief.*
Dimetri Mgaloblichvily,
Toma Baramidzi,
Miron Tschonia, Ermile Antadzi,
Ivan Baramidzi,
Loucas Tschartishvily,
Michael Antadzi,
Vladimir Jacutahvily.

## ARABS.
Sheik Hadji Tahar, *Chief.*
Hadji Cheriff, *Whirling Dervish.*

Moly Ambark,
Ameen Abou Hamed,
M. Muzie,
H. Abachi,
Mohammed Agram,
Hadji Hamid,

Oshan,
Masand,
Nagim Abdullah,
Nageeb Ballish,
Willie Masand,
Brodie ben Hadji,
Togler ben Hadji.

## CUBANS.
Col. Mariano Aymerich, *Chief.*
Lieut. Evaristo M. Alonso.
Lieut. Andres Fontanilla.
Antonio Marti, Manuel Portuondo,
Rafael Rodriguez, Ramon Ferreno,
Benito Carreras.

## HAWAIIANS.
David Kipi,
J. Kulia,
G. Makalina,

K. Natsia,
W. Hopili,
Isabella Pary,
Ribaka Natsia.

## FILIPINOS.
Felix Alcantara, Geronimo Momo,
Isidora Alcantara.

## INDIANS.
### CHIEFS.
Iron Tail,
Black Fox,

Growler,
Iron Cloud,
Has No Horse.

### BRAVES
Spotted Weasel,
Good Horse,
Comes Out Holy,
Flying Horse,
John Kills Brave,
Standing Soldier,
White Bird,
Little Bull,
Comes Last,
Comes Out Bear,
Richard Lip,
Spotted Horse Fight,
White Bonnet,
Kills in Loge,
Comes Killing,
Holy Bear,

Sam Stabber,
White Belly,
Eagle Fox,
Pluck Porcupine,
Red Calf,
Jacob Iron Eagle,
Charging Thunder,
Dreamer,
Wounded,
Lound Thunder,
Frank Meat,
Albert Thunder Hawk,
Ed. Porcupine Knee,
Sam Lone Bear,
Mounted Sheep,
Whirlwind Horse,
Kills Enemy.

### SQUAWS.
Mary Kills Enemy, Jennie Spotted Horse,
White Cow.

### PAPOOSE.
Willie White Bird.

### INTERPRETER.
David Bull Bear.

### WATCHMAN OF INDIAN CAMP.
J.J. Ryan

## "BRONCHO" STABLE.
W.W. Reedy *in Charge.*

J.F. Meade,
Hugh Harkins, ............... Cowboy String
Jas. Bass, ................. English Lancers
M.T. McKenzie, ................ Rough Riders
Naber E. Smith, ................. U.S. Cavalry
Geo. Bare, ........................ Mexican
Dan White, ......... Hawaiians and Filipinos
Al Hook, ........................... Cossack
Wm. Jones, ........................... Arab.
Chris Peterson, .................... German
Chas. Judd,
Sam. Harkins, .................... Artillery
Marshall Ochoa,
W. Dryer, ......................... Indian
Dewitt Genung,
Chas. Kelly,
J.W. Porter, ........................ Mules
Russell Churchill, ......... Bucking Horses
Giess Stine, ........... Col. Cody's Stock
Jas. Murphy, ....... Col. Cody's Coachman
J.R. Ziegler, ...... Driver of "Buffalo" Wagon
Harry Murphy, ...... In Charge of Buffaloes

## "WILD WEST" BLACKSMITHS
Fred Kurz, Joseph Ferren

## WARDROBE AND PROPERTIES
Chas. Wichelhausen.
Chas J. Ansert, Wm. Monday,
Jas. Fish, Martin Dillon.

## AMMUNITION.
Wm. Smith *in Charge.*
Tom Edwards, Roy Myers,
Jas. Berger.

## BAGGAGE STOCK.
Chas. Evans, *Superintendent.*
Wm. McNaul, *Assistant.*

## EIGHT-HORSE DRIVERS.
**DRIVER.** **HELPER.**
Jas. Thomas, Henry White,
Perry Camp, Andy Johnson,
S.W. Elliott, Chas. Miller,
David Denio, Chas. Foley.

## SIX-HORSE DRIVERS.
Ed. Miller, Jas. Robinson,
Wm. Montgomery, Grant Hulvey,
Chas. Mitchell, Jas. McGovern,
Harry E. Mills.

## FOUR-HORSE DRIVERS.
Jas. Afford, Jas. Williams,
Sam Woodman, Wm. Donohue.
John Gallagher, J.F. Tewell,
Geo. Eastman, Rob't Burns.

## PULL-UP TEAMS.
John Laird, Chas. Cook,
Thos. Lee.

## BUGGY STOCK.
Jack Lewis.

## LEAD BARS AND BODY POLES.
Frank Emery.

## FEED.
John Puget.

## BLACKSMITH AND REPAIR DEPARTMENT.
Dan Taylor, *Master Mechanic.*
Fred Keller, .................... Carpenter.
E.J. Collins, ............... Harness Maker.
John Norbury, .................. Blacksmith
Alex. Young, ................... Blacksmith

## RAILROAD DEPARTMENT.
John McLaughlin, *Master of Transportation*
R.P. Murphy, *Assistant*
John Rose, ............... Car Inspector
A.H. Miller, .......... Watchman 1st Section
Joe Brown, .......... Watchman 2nd Section
Wm. Remack, ............... Chandeliers
Paul Spearing,
Frank Arnett, .................... Polers

## TRAINMEN.
Frank Coyle, A.E. Meyer,
L.D. Bottariff, John Bennett,
John Fallon, Jere Murphy.

## SPECIAL WATCHMEN.
John Stacks, .......... White Ticket Wagon
Frank Quinn, ............... Private Office
M. Hogan, ............... 2d Section Stock

### CAR PORTERS

John Noble, *Head Porter.*
Wm. Vogel, Car 51,    Pete Wallace, Car 54,
Geo. Long, Car 52,    Chas. Carroll, Car 55
Harry Gears, Car 53,    F.C. Hawley, Car 56,
Wm. Reilly, Car 57.

### COL. CODY'S PRIVATE CAR NO. 50.

Alfred Heimer, *Porter,*
W.L. Brown, *Cook.*

### SIDE-SHOW

Messrs. Drew & Campbell, *Managers.*

### PERFORMERS AND CURIOS.

Ashida and Koh, .............. Japanese Magic
Olga, .................... Snake Enchantress
Wm. Baker, ..................... Boy Giant
Chemah and Pearl Robinson, ........ Midgets
J.G. Sheidler, ................ King of Cards
Balbroma, ..................... Fire King
Victoria, ................. Sword-swallower
Val Vino, ..................... Juggler
Millie Owen, ............. Long-haired Lady
Prince Oskazuma, ........... Kaffir Warrior
Ben Casper,
W.F. Greiner, } ........ Venetian Glass Blowers
J. McClellan,
Ben Powell, } Electrograph and Mind-readers

### LECTURER

Burt Davis.

### ORATORS.

P.J. Staunton,    Jos. F. Ferris,
Frank Cloud.

### DOOR TENDER.

Frank Quinn.

### SIDE-SHOW CANVASMEN.

H.E. Tudor, *Superintendent.*
Wm. Powers,    J. Martin,
Wm. Allen,    Geo. Fuller,
Jno. McLean.
Harry Tudor, ....................... Inside.

### SIDE-SHOW BAND.

L. Sacketts, *Leader.*
F. Rechhia, ................... B♭ Clarinet
F. Donato, .................... E♭ Clarinet
G. Grella, ................ Solo B♭ Cornet
A. Scerni, ................. First B♭ Cornet
E. Renzi, ..................... B♭ Baritone
L.D. Paolo, ................... B♭ Trombone
W. Pellazzo, .................... E♭ Alto
D. Zuglielmo, ................... Bass Drum
D. Barbieri, .................... Small Drum

### CONFECTIONERY DEP'T.

Chas. L. Ramsey, *Superintendent.*
S.H. Davis, *Assistant.*
C.W. Spadi *in Charge of Supplies.*

### BUTCHERS.

C.E. Fearn,    C.E. Brooks,
Harry Merrick,    Fred Roteman,
Jas. White,    Arthur W. Horton,
Joe Burke,    Garrett Henry,
A. Watt,    Lou C. Cloud.

### NEW ENGLAND POP-CORN FACTORY.

M.C. Bowers.

### CONCERT COMPANY.

"The Ramseys," .............. Comedy Duo.
Bessie Searles, ................. Serio-Comic
Schafer and Read, .......... Musical Comedy
Cloud and Kershaw, ........ Irish Comedians
"The Brannigans," ............. Jig Dancers
Nellie Waters, ................ Comedianne

### CONCERT ORCHESTRA

J. Schilling, .................... First Violin
Ed. Weber, .................... Second Violin
Wm. A. Frank, ....................... Viola
M.A. McAdams, ..................... Bass
F. Genter, ....................... Clarionet
A. Ziehm, ....................... Cornet
L. Williams, .................... Trombone

### OFFICIAL PROGRAMMES.

J. & H. Mayer, *Publishers.*
Tom Burke *in Charge.*
H. Mayer, *Solicitor.*

### AGENTS.

Wm. Conroy,    Frank Clear,
Walter Miller,    Ed O'Connell.
Geo. Manchester,
Agent for "Buffalo Bill's" History

### OFFICIAL PROGRAMMES.

### ELECTRICAL DEPARTMENT.

M. B. Bailey, *Superintendent.*
D. MacDonald, *Chief Electrician.*
Wm. J. Connor, *Chief Engineer.*

### FIREMEN.

Archie Clements,    Wm. M. Penn.

### ASSISTANTS.

Maurice Doody,    Joe McCann,
Geo. H. Gooch,    Bernie McBride,
Henry Reever,    Larry Murphy.

### CALCIUM LIGHTS

Maurice Doody,    Geo. H. Gooch.

### CHANDELIERS.

Jack Cullen *in Charge.*
Ed. A. Combs, *Assistant.*

### CANVAS DEPARTMENT.

Jake Platt, *Superintendent.*
John Eberle, *First Assistant.*
David Jarrett, *Second Assistant.*
Jack Dawson, *Horse Tents.*
Wm. Smithey, *Dressing Room and Backing.*
Jas McCaffrey,    M. Mack,
John Condon,    Larry Sullivan,
John White,    Wm. Cronin,
L. Callahan,    John Murphy,
Sam Maitland,    Wm. Hunter,
Herbert Parkes,    Mike Jones,
Ed Barry,    John Weaver,
Wm. Hutton,    Ed Howard,
John Halpin,    Pat Burke,
Mike Burns,    Lee Fuller,
Andy Wood,    Thos. Ryan,
Geo. Davis,    M. Quinlan,
Alex. McFrine,    Larry Eagan,
Walter King,    Wm. Murphy,
Lyman Mayo,    Wm. Thomas,
Mike McManus,    Jos. Collins,
Wm. Sampson,    Geo. Amos,
Chas. Lavesta,    Chas. Vanberg,
Geo. Smith,    Ernest Yelland,
Wm. Arnold,    Edward Bitting,
Chris Cair,    Geo. Pratt,
Jos. Trempley,    Mike Keating,
Thos. Foley,    John Walsh,
Harry Buckner,    Jack Bryan,
John D. Fulton,    John Morrow,
John Bergeman,    Jas. Harrison,
John Tracy,    John Rassler,
Harry Peterson,    Harry Hoskins,
Unix Robia,    John Bauersis,
Geo. Hunt.

### FRONT END.

John A. Eberle, *Superintendent.*

### SEATS.

Jas. McCaffrey, *in Charge.*
John Condon, *Assistant.*
John White, *Leveler.*

### JACK SETTERS.

Bob Callahan,    Herbert Parkes,
Sam Maitland,    Wm. Hutton,
Hugh Gallagher.

### TOE-PIN DRIVERS.

John Halpin,    Andy Wood,
Ed Barry,    Geo. Davis,
Mike Burns,    Alex. McFrine.

### BLOCKS.

Lyman Mayo.

### KIDS.

Walter King.

### BACK END.

Dave Jarrett, *Superintendent.*

### SEATS.

M. Mack *in Charge.*
Larry Sullivan, *Assistant.*
Wm. Hunter, *Leveler.*
Mike Jones, *Toe Leveler.*

### JACK SETTERS.

John Weaver,    Pat. Burke,
Ed. Howard,    Lee Fuller,
Thos. Ryan.

### TOE-PIN DRIVERS

Larry Egan,    Mike McManus,
Wm. Murphy,    Wm. Sampson,
Wm. Thomas,    Chas. Lavesta.

### BLOCKS.

Geo. Smith.

### KIDS.

Wm. Murphy.

### RESERVED SEATS

M. Quinlan *in Charge.*

### STRINGER SETTERS.

Wm. Arnold,    Chris Cair.

### JACK SETTERS.

Jos. Trempley,    Thos. Foley,
Wm. Murphy,    Harry Buckner.

### TOE-PIN DRIVERS.

Harry Hoskins,    John Rossler,
Ed Daily,    Wm. Ryan.

### BLOCKS.

Chas. Vanberg.

### KIDS.

Jos. Collins.

### BIG TOP STAKE AND CHAIN, Nos. 6 and 11.

John Murphy,    Wm. Cronin.

### HORSE TENTS.

John Dawson, *Superintendent.*
Wm. Ryan,    Unix Robia,
John Tracey,    Ed Dailey,
Geo. Amos,    Harry Peterson,
John Rassler,    Harry Buckner,
John Welsh,    Thos. Foley,
Jas. Harrison,    Thos. Murphy,
Wm. Carey,    Harry Hoskins.

### STAKE WAGON No. 14.

John Walsh.

### BACKING AND DRESSING ROOM.

Wm. Smithey, *Superintendent.*

**RIGHT CURTAIN.**
John Bauereis,     Geo. Hunt.

**CENTER CURTAIN.**
Edward Bitting,     John Bergeman,
Ernest Yelland,     John Morrow.

**LEFT CURTAIN.**
Jack Bryan,     John D. Fulton.

**FRONT-DOOR MEN.**
Geo. Pratt,     Mike Keating.

**SAIL MAKERS.**
John Weaver,     Geo. Halpin,
John Walsh.

**COOK HOUSE.**
Messrs. Keen & Langan, *Caterers.*
Chas. W. Petty, *Advance.*
Fred Bowman, *Accountant for Wild West.*
Sam. T. Bitmead,
    *Accountant for Keen & Langan.*

**COOKS.**
Wm. Myers, *Head Cook.*
Harry Holmes,     Henry Hiler,
John Hammond.

**BUTCHER.**
Chas. Felix.

**CAMPFIRE.**
Mike Connelly.

**WAITERS.**
M. Martin, *Head Waiter.*
Wm. Walsh, *Assistant Head Waiter.*

**TABLE No. 1—STAFF.**
Fred. Adams,     Eddie Walton,
Thos. Rafferty, Coffee-boy.

**TABLE No. 2—COWBOYS AND BAND.**
H. Stewart,     Jos. McCaffrey,
Joe Gillin, Coffee-boy.

**TABLE NO. 3—PRIVILEGE.**
Jas. Kelly,     W. Sproegal.

**TABLE No. 4—ARABS, ETC.**
J. Coleman,     H. Bird,
G. Packett.

**TABLE NO. 5—AMERICAN SOLDIERS.**
C. Hutchinson,     J. Hobson,
B. Palmer, Coffee-boy.

**TABLE NO. 6—ENGLISH AND GERMAN SOLDIERS.**
N. Nist,     Chas. Black,
J. Ruffells, Coffee-boy.

**TABLE NO. 7—INDIANS.**
J. Furlong.

**WORKMEN'S TABLES Nos. 8, 9 AND 10.**
C. Carson,     C. Whitney,
W. Binne,     Wm. Ives,
W. Wagstaffe,     Wm. Basman.
Jas. Knight, Coffee-boys.
John Kehoe,

**DESSERT BOYS.**
L. Routledge,     Bert Cohn.

**DISHWASHERS.**
Jesse Jackson,     Jos. Jackson.

**LAUNDRYMAN.**
D. McMillan.

**NIGHT WATCHMEN.**
Chas. Nicholson,     Thos. Devine.

**NIGHT-LUNCH STAND.**
Tom Austin.

**ORDER OF PARADE.**

**COL. W.F. CODY,**
    (Buffalo Bill)

**OUT RIDERS.** Wild West Band No. 1, in wagon.
Sioux Indians.

**J.D. TIPPETTS.** German Garde-Kurassiers of His Majesty, Kaiser Wilhelm II.
Electric Light Engine, No. 1.
A Group of Riffian Arabs.
Arapahoe Indians.
Filipino Rough Riders.

**JOHNNIE BAKER.** Russian Cossacks.
Sixteenth English Lancers,
    (Queen's Own.)
A Squad of Hawaiians.
Indian Squaws.
Indian Boy Chiefs.
South American Gauchos.

**JOHN FRANZ.** Famous Cowboy Band,
    Mounted,
    Wm. Sweeney, Leader.
Col. Teddy B. Roosevelt's
    Rough Riders.
Burlè Indians.
A Group of Mexicans.
Electric Light Engine, No. 2
A Band of Cuban Insurgents.
Cheyenne Indians.

**JOE ESQUIVELL.** Old Deadwood Stage Coach.
American Cowboys.
Wild West Band No. 3,
    on Chariot Tableaux.
Sixth U.S. Cavalry.
Detachment Fifth U.S.
    Artillery, Battery D.

**OFFICIAL PROGRAMME.**

1—**Overture,** "Star Spangled Banner," Cowboy Band, Wm. Sweeney, Leader.

2—**Grand Review,** introducing the Rough Riders of the World—Indians, Cowboys, Mexicans, Cossacks, Gauchos, Arabs, Scouts, Guides and detachments of fully-equipped Regular Soldiers of the Armies of America, England, Germany and Russia, a Color Guard of Cuban Veterans, and a squad of Hawaiian, Puerto Rican and Filipino Rough Riders.

3—**Miss Annie Oakley,** Celebrated Shot, who will illustrate her dexterity in the use of firearms.

4—**Race of Races.** Race between a Cowboy, a Cossack, a Mexican, an Arab, a Goucho, and an Indian, on Spanish-Mexican, Bronco, Russian, Indian and Arabian Horses.

5—**U.S. Artillery Drill,** by veterans from Capt. Thorpe's Battery D, Fifth Regiment. U.S. Artillery.

6—**Illustrating a Prairie Emigrant Train Crossing the Plains.** It is attacked by marauding Indians who are in turn repulsed by "Buffalo Bill" and a number of Scouts and Cowboys.

7—**Pony Express.** A former Pony Post Rider will show how letters and telegrams of the Republic were distributed across our Continent previous to the building of railways and telegraph.

8—**A Group of Mexicans** from Old Mexico will illustrate the use of the lasso and perform various feats of horsemanship.

9—**The Battle of San Juan Hill.** Introducing detachments from Roosevelt's Rough Riders, Twenty-fourth Infantry, Ninth and Tenth Cavalry, Grimes' Battery, Garcia's Cuban Couts, Pack Train, etc., etc.

SCENE 1—A halt on the Road to San Juan.

(Several hours are supposed to elapse before the opening of the second scene.)

SCENE 2—Storming of the Hill.

10—**A Group of Riffian Arab Horsemen** will illustrate their style of horsemanship, together with native sports and pastimes.

11—**Johnny Baker,** Celebrated Young American Marksman.

12—**Cossacks,** from the Caucasus of Russia, in feats of horsemanship, native dances, etc.

13—**Gymkana Race.** Riders gallop, dismount, turn coat inside out, remount, gallop, dismount, light cigar, put up umbrella, mount and come in with umbrella up and cigar lighted.

14—**Cowboy Fun.** Picking objects from the ground, lassoing wild horses, riding the buckers, etc.

15—**Indians** from the Sioux, Arapahoe, Burlè and Cheyenne tribes will illustrate the Indian mode of fighting, war dances and games.

16—**Military Musical Drill,** by a detachment from the 16th Lancers (Queen's Own), British Army, and a detachment from the Garde-Kurassiers of His Majesty Kaiser Wilhelm II.

17—**Sixth United States Cavalry.** Veterans from Col. Sumner's celebrated regiment at Ft. Meyer, Va., in military exercises, and an exhibition of athletic sports and horsemanship.

NOTE.—The men will wear the uniforms adopted by the United States Army on the frontier. The horses are Western range horses, used in this manner for the first time in history. The Army and National Guard use the "American" horse.

18—**Attack on the Deadwood Mail Coach by Indians,** repulse of the Indians and rescue of the stage, passengers and mail, by "Buffalo Bill" and his attendant Cowboys.

19—**Racing by Indian Boys on Bareback Horses.**

20—**Three Minutes With the Rough Riders of the World.**

21—**Col. W.F. CODY** ("Buffalo Bill") in his unique feats of sharpshooting while riding at full speed.

22—**Buffalo Hunt,** as it was in the Far West of North America, by "Buffalo Bill" and Indians exhibiting the last of the only known native herd of buffalo.

23—**Attack on Settlers' Cabin** and rescue by "Buffalo Bill" and a band of Cowboys, Scouts and Frontiersmen.

24—**Salute,** by the entire company.

**THE ANNUAL SPRING OPENING.**

The show was moved from "Ambrose Park" to Madison Square Garden for the opening of the season on Sunday, March 26th. The parade which was to have taken place on Tuesday, 28th, had to be postponed until the following day on account of inclement weather.

The first performance was given on Wednesday night, March 29th, before a crowded house. Several entirely new features were introduced in the programme, the chief being "The Battle of San Juan," which proved an instantaneous success.

On Friday, April 7th, the afternoon performance was given for the benefit of the orphans and inmates of the different asylums and institutions around New York. Altogether, thirty-one performances were given during the stay in the Garden, at each of which the Garden was well filled, while on several occasions the doors had to be closed for the night performance. The season proved the most successful ever given in New York.

The cowboy band that traveled with the Wild West Show. Buffalo Bill's Cowboy Band, William Sweeney, conductor, 1887-1913. They wore gray shirts, slouched hats, and moccasins, rode matched horses on parade, and played a half-hour concert of classical music preceding the performance.

Part of the Wild West troop visit Grant's tomb. The show introduced the Wild West to the world, and it also gave the participants a chance to see the world.

Chief Joseph (in white jacket) was one of the last War Chiefs to give up his fight with the white man. Once a feared enemy, he now visited the Wild West Show.

Likewise, balanced against the exhibitions of skill and the ceremonials that pictured the Indians as men of talent and virtue were the scenes of savagery — the attacks on emigrant trains, the Deadwood stage coach, and the settler's cabin.

## UNANNOUNCED, NEW THRILLER THRILLS AT "WILD WEST"

### "Buffalo Bill" and "Pawnee Bill" Exhibit a High Diver Who Spurns Water Landing.

Unannounced, the management of the Buffalo Bill's Wild West and Pawnee Bill's Far East combination show at Madison Square Garden last night at the opening put on the greatest of thrillers.

It was called "Fresiso." A slim youth was pulled up to the topmost steel rafters and, diving forty feet through space, landed on a soap-stoned slide and, landing on his feet, ran, waving his hand to the audience. There is nothing faked or mechanical about this. It leaves the automobile loop the loop and other thrillers far behind. Nothing like it has ever been seen here before.

For years the Buffalo Bill show has been an annual part of New York city's life. It is better than ever this year, Aug...

## KING AND QUEEN AT WILD WEST SHOW.

### Take Children and Grandchildren to See the Rough Riders and Indians.

### PRINCE "EDDY," FUTURE KING, NOW ASKS FOR A LASSO.

### Alexandra Specially Interested in Little Redskins, Edward in Riders and Shooters.

(Copyright, 1903, by the Press Publishing Company, New York World.)
(Special Cable Despatch to The World.)
LONDON, March 14.—Her Majesty does not look a day older than when she rode in the Deadwood coach in 1887. Col. W. F. Cody ("Buffalo Bill") declared to-night. "She is the most beautiful woman living. She is too good ever to get old."

Queen Alexandra had visited the Wild West Show in...

## CLEVELAND PLAIN DEALER

### JUN 1 1908

## HISTORY OF WORLD FLASHED IN ARENA

### Search Earth's Far Corners for Strange Races to Ride With Buffalo Bill.

### Indians, Cossacks, Arabs and Freaks Break Bread in Harmony.

Twice a day one of the greatest of modern historians produces an illustrated history of the world. Not a pale, anemic, bookish thing like Ridpath, or John Fiske, or Mr. Herodotus, or Froissart, or any of that aggregation. No, siree.

It's the story, of the sturdier races of men, of bloody warfare, of shield and spear and tomahawk and Winchester; of action and horses, and the kind of adventure romance which doesn't itself in sighing swains and note paper; the kind that shakes the dice with death and to the end.

It's the story of times are where wages and rent and action and south export telephones ar ndicitis do

## WILD WEST SHOW OPENS AT GARDEN

### Col. William F. Cody Again Introduces His Congress of Rough Riders of the World.

### MAJOR-GEN. CARR IS PRESENT

### A Number of New Features, Including a Prairie Fire and an Avalanche.

Except for a bad case of wind colic, which caused breezes to waft where a hurricane was supposed to blow, and which also caused the avalanche to remain inert and harmless, whereas it was supposed to do a whole lot of damage, Buffalo Bill's Wild West Show opened most auspiciously last evening at Madison Square Garden.

And it was not the management's fault that the startling new spectacle, an avalanche in action, was displayed only in part. It was the electrician's, and the disappointment of last night is not likely to be repeated again this season.

Another new feature, and one which also depends upon elect...

## OLYMPIA REVISITED BY ROYALTY.

### AN EXCITING MOMENT.

### "MOSES" AND THE KING'S UMBRELLA

Colonel Cody and his Wild West Show have d a great compliment paid them. On Saturday afternoon the Queen, with the King, several other members of the Royal Family, were pectators of the Congress of Rough Riders; and her Majesty was so pleased with the experience that yesterday afternoon she revisited Olympia, accompanied by the Prince and Princess of Wales, Princess Victoria, Princess Mary of Wales, and Princesses Victoria and Patricia of Connaught. Those in attendance on the Royal party were Lord and Lady Mary Lygon, Commander Godfrey Faussett, Sir Arthur Bigge, and General Sir Stanley Clarke.

The immense audience gave noisy demonstrati enthusiasm when the august visitors utiful Royal box. The perform

## Evening Express.

### Monday, May 11, 1903.

### BISHOP'S ADDRESS TO THE WILD WEST SHOWMEN.

### Interesting Service on the Show Ground.

### REMARKABLE SPECTACLE.

A novel and picturesque event took place at the Wild West Show yesterday, when the Bishop of Liverpool (Dr. Chavasse) preached a sermon on the showground. The intimation of his lordship's desire to address the performers in the exhibition caused great pleasure to all concerned, and his visit was anticipated with keen interest among the diversified peoples represented in "Buffalo Bill's" unique collection. This was shown by the large assembly of those who voluntarily attended the service. Except for a few invited guests the attendance consisted exclusively of the performers, of whom some hundreds were present. These were accommodated at one end of the arena, and a curious mo'ey gathering they made. At the from Cody ("Buffalo Bill") was seat were also present Mr. Major Jno. M. Burk officials.

## KING AND QUEEN SEE "BUFFALO BILL"

### Their Majesties, with Ambassador Choate and Party as Guests, Visit "Wild West."

LONDON, Saturday.—King Edward, Queen Alexandra, the Princess Victoria, Prince and Princess Charles of Denmark and three of the children of the Prince of Wales, all attended their suites, occupied a specially val box at the Olympia this to thoroughly enjoy

Mr. Choate White

## WILD WEST GIVES TAMER EAST THRILLS

### Some 8,000 in Madison Square Garden Watch Buffalo Bill's Big Show.

### REALISTIC PRAIRIE FIRE A GREAT NEW FEATURE.

'Tame East went to Wild West last night in Madison Square Garden, and entered so heartily into the spirit of the "wild and woolly" that Buffalo Bill, after listening to the delighted yells of more than eight thousand spectators, said there were more Indians in New York than he had ever met beyond the Mississippi.

Men and women who almost had forgotten the thrilling tales of read in other d the realistic sce 'ill's latest rel There was

## WILD WEST IS HERE

### Buffalo Bill's Troupe Has First Dress Rehearsal.

### VETERAN SCOUT IN SADDLE

### Men From the Wild West and Far East Practice Their Parts.

### SCENES AT SHOW GROUNDS

### Greatest Hustling Needed to Get Everything in Readiness for the Afternoon's Entertainment.

## "THE WILD WEST" IN BIRMINGHAM.

### OPENING PERFORMANCES.

There are few people in Birmingham, young or old, who will not be deeply interested in Buffalo Bill's "Wild West" show, which is now on a fortnight's visit to Birmingham. Who among us has not been thrilled in his youth whoe reading of the stirring adventures of the heroes of Fennimore Cooper and other writers of fiction dealing with life in the "Wild West," or the backwoods of America—heroes who have passed their days as trappers of "fur," hunters of the buffalo, or as sharing in the perils of their fellows and the American soldiers in their fights with the Red Indians. The march of civilisation has been such that hunting on the prairie is now very limited, and the perils of warfare are practically unknown, but the deeds of old remain in our memories, thanks to the novelist, and the realism of the incidents so graphically described nment by Buffalo Bill

## INDIANS WIN GAME IN WILD WEST SHOW

### Football on Horseback Feature of Buffalo Bill's Opening at Madison Square Garden.

Buffalo Bill's Indians and cowboys played football on horseback at Madison Square Garden last night, and the Indians won by two goals. The six thousand people who had gathered to see the opening of the Buffalo Bill Wild West show for a short season applauded the cowboys loudest when the game began, but the first half had not ended before they were rooting for the red men. When the game was over they applauded until

## UTICA DAILY PRESS

### BUFFALO BILL IS IN TOWN

### WILD WEST IS IN UTICA TO-DAY

### Many Persons Visited the Grounds Yesterday and Saw the Big Show From the Inside—Many New Features Offered This Year, Including Foot Ball on Horseback—How Performers Live.

When a Press reporter took a trip across the New York Central tracks yesterday afternoon and from there went into the circus grounds where Buffalo Bill put up his tents during the morning, he was given an opportunity to see how the show looked from the inside. Fred M. Hall, press agent for the big

## Evening Express.

### Monday, May 11, 1903.

### BISHOP'S ADDRESS TO THE WILD WEST SHOWMEN.

### Interesting Service on the Show Ground.

### REMARK...SPECTACLE.

"Buck" Taylor —
Champion Cowboy

His "act" most resembled that of the present day rodeo. He rode broncs, calf roped and excelled in steer wrestling.

Cody continually improved the Wild West, adding new acts to it, keeping only the best from the previous years. He always retained exhibitions of cowboy and Indian skills and portraits of Western history.

Cowboy performers in the 1895 Wild West Show. J. Esquival, Jim Kid, Jim Mitchell, Dick Johnson, Billy Bullock, Tony Esquival, Johnny Baker, Joe Pshirrer.

Buffalo Bill and royalty on the Deadwood stage in London, England, 1887.

Next to the herd of buffalo, the most important property of the Buffalo Bill Wild West Show was the delapidated deadwood mail coach. For many a season it was pursued by yelling Indians.

The coach saw service on the line between Deadwood, South Dakota and Cheyenne, Wyoming before it was acquired by Buffalo Bill in 1883.

With superb showmanship, Cody would invite distinguished members of the audience to ride in the coach to its destined attack by Indians. When the show played an 1887 command performance at Windsor Castle in England to celebrate Queen Victoria's Golden Jubilee, the Prince of Wales rode shotgun as Buffalo Bill drove his passengers (the Kings of Greece, Saxony, Denmark, and Belgium) to safety while the U.S. Cavalry repelled a bloodcurdling attack by Wild West renegades.

Squaw Man Nelson and his Indian family. Nelson was the Driver of the Deadwood Stage.

Show Bill

The 1899 Wild West program, describing the frontiersmen who were in the show, summed it all up:

"... They are truly and exceptionally historic, heroic and romantic characters. They should be seen of all men, for they are a type that time shall know no more."

Gordon Lillie — Pawnee Bill — became Cody's partner in 1909. His influence tended to make the Wild West more like a circus, the difference grew negligible in later years. Starting in 1898, he added sideshow attractions — a snake charmer, a sword swallower, a boy giant, a Kaffir warrior, jugglers, midgets, Venetian glass blowers — upon the advice of his new partner.

Cody and Lillie were partners in the "Two Bill" show, "Buffalo Bill's Wild West and Pawnee Bill's Great Far East Show." Despite the fact that Gene Fowler in his book "Timberline" intimated the arrangement was a cumbersome alliance for Buffalo Bill, Major Lillie declares that the show, since 1908 had been clearing from $100,000 to $300,000 annually until 1913 when it was wrecked. Mayor Gordon Lillie "Pawnee Bill" and Buffalo Bill combined shows in 1908. Bill with Pawnee Bill, surrounded by elephants and Indians. These later dimensions, bizarre and perhaps cheapening, foreshadowed the day in 1913 when Cody, in financial stress, was forced to merge with the Sells-Floto Circus.

Cody and friends welcome visitors to the new Memorial Museum at the main entrance.

*Come as you are* — part of the daily crowd that get a glimpse of the true Wild West.

Museum exhibit showing items from Cody's years as an actor.

Among his many honors was this one of Knighthood by the Italian Government.

Cody was surrounded by famous people out of our history.

Among the museum's newest acquisitions are these detailed models of horse-drawn carriages and utility wagons sculptured by Denver artist Ed Wittrock. These scaled down models are the only ones in existence since they had been created exclusively for the Buffalo Bill Memorial Museum.

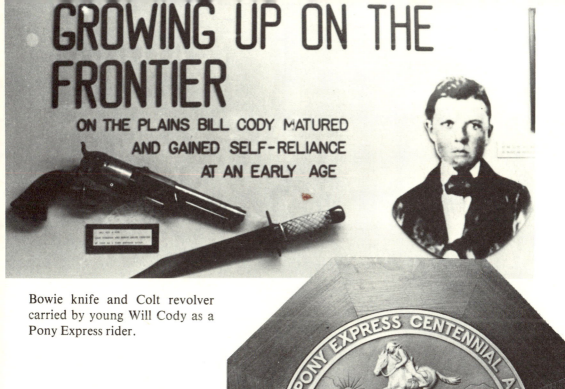

# GROWING UP ON THE FRONTIER

## ON THE PLAINS BILL CODY MATURED AND GAINED SELF-RELIANCE AT AN EARLY AGE

Bowie knife and Colt revolver carried by young Will Cody as a Pony Express rider.

Plaque commemorating the Pony Express.

At 14, Bill Cody became a Pony Express rider. His usual run was 76 miles per day but he once reached a relay station, found the relief rider had been killed and kept on riding for a total 322 mile roundtrip.

The Pony Express existed for only 17 months and might have been completely forgotten if Buffalo Bill hadn't included it in his Wild West for more than 30 years, performing before "... millions of Americans and Europeans ... forever riveting this drama in our history and legend as a uniquely American experience."

Much of Buffalo Bill's fancy trappings are on display at the museum. He was a trend setter in Western Style.

Col. Cody's favorite saddle.

He experienced an unsuccessful year of gold prospecting in Colorado, after which he became a Pony Express rider. When the Civil War broke out, Cody joined the Jayhawkers, an armed band of anti-slavery men in Kansas.

Museum display of Buffalo Bill momentos.

Cody was eight years old when his family moved from his birthplace near Davenport Iowa to Kansas. His father died three years later, and the 11-year-old boy started down the path of becoming a storied American, first as a mounted messenger for a wagon freight company.

The museum is part of the Denver Parks and Recreation Department. Shown are Jim Dixon, Superintendent of Denver Mountain Parks, C. P. Fox, Counselor, and Curator Stan Zamonski.

Museum exhibits of Cody as an army scout.

Museum exhibit of Buffalo Bill the hunter.

Buffalo Bill's grave and the original museum building.

"At Rest Here by His Request," is the epitaph inscribed on a tombstone on top of Lookout Mountain where Col. William Frederick "Buffalo Bill" Cody lies at rest. The tomb was blasted out of the rock.

GRAVESITE — The impressive burial site of "Buffalo Bill" Cody and his wife Louisa is exquisitely set on Lookout Mountain overlooking Denver on one side and the canyons and valleys of the mountains on the other. The American flag flies majestically above the grave honoring the exploit of Colonel Cody.

Pahaska Tepee Museum — The original Memorial Museum, in 1925, as Johnny Baker and his wife built it. Part of the building is still in use as a snack bar and gift shop. There is a breath-taking view from the observation deck.

A scene inside the old Pahaska Tepee Museum. Pahaska was the Indian word for long hair, a name applied to Cody.

Johnny Baker surrounded by Indian Chiefs during their visit to Buffalo Bill's grave.

Annually 700,000 visitors pay tribute at Buffalo Bill's Grave on Lookout Mountain near Denver.

The Buffalo Bill Riding Club annual floral presentation at the grave site.

The museum houses numerous fine paintings, many of which came out of Cody's own extensive Western Collection. He was one of the first avid collectors of American Western art.

A little known fact about 'Buffalo Bill' Cody is that he was one of the first and foremost collectors of western art. At a time when most art critics and dealers were mainly interested in European masters, Col. Cody was supporting many American artists.

Fredric Remington was a constant guest of Codys'. Today one of his paintings completed during a visit entitled THE RANCH HAND signed and dated "Fredric Remington to Col. W.F. Cody '99, Big Horn Basin" hangs in the museum.

BISON HEAD and HERD OF BUFFALO by E.W. Linders, were presented to Cody by the artist, Jan. 28, 1912. As was THE BEST KNOWN MAN IN THE COUNTRY a bust portrait of the Colonel.

Two paintings by St. G. Stanley are signed and dated by the artist as early as June, 1876.

One of the most valued paintings of the museum collection is an oil painting by C.S. Stobie, entitled THE LIFE I LOVE showing Cody riding into a hunting camp.

There are two paintings by H.H. Cross of very fine quality dated Aug. 25, 1908, which have added historic element to the museum collection.

CODY THE SCOUT by a lesser known artist, Pappacena, dated 1892, is said to have been Buffalo Bill's favorite painting of himself. It was presented as a gift from Mrs. Cody to the City of Denver.

There is a handsome oil portrait of Cody as a young man executed by the famous Philadelphia artist J. Knox O'Neil.

"Buffalo Hunt" By J. Gogolin 1926

    Among the many artists represented are Bell Renz, E.W. Deming, R. Farrington Elwell, Paul Warner, Claud Frasier and the English painter Edward Thoni. Paul Gregg, the well known illustrator for many years with The Denver Post is represented with two renditions of Buffalo Bill's Grave.

    It was Buffalo Bill who encouraged Charley Schreyvogel by giving him the run of the Wild West during it's Eastern appearances. Later Cody invited Schreyvogel as an honored guest at his ranches in Nebraska and Wyoming.

    The artist Jacob Gogolin's seven paintings comprise the largest collection of all the artists represented. He was a close bosom friend of Buffalo Bill's during his last years in Denver. Born in Germany, Gogolin (1864-1940) came to this country in 1902 and spent most of his life in Denver. Gogolin, together with Cody and Henry Zietz, the owner of the historic Buckhorn Exchange Restaurant, formed a threesome that frequented the popular places in Denver.

    Gogolin never became nationally famous although some of his oil paintings are as fine as any in the collection. Not all of his paintings are accounted for, but besides those that the museum has and a few that hang in St. Anthonys' Hospital, there are a number at the Kansas State Historical Society in Topeka, Kansas.

This equestrian figure "The Scout" was painted by Pappacena in 1889. It occupies a prominent place in the Art Gallery.

"Buffalo Bill" (Col. Wm. F. Cody) on his favorite horse, Isham, as he appeared in his last public performance in 1916.

Teddy Roosevelt, on hearing of Buffalo Bill's death, described him as embodying "courage, strength and self-reliant hardihood which are vital to the well-being of the nation."

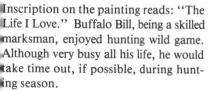

Inscription on the painting reads: "The Life I Love." Buffalo Bill, being a skilled marksman, enjoyed hunting wild game. Although very busy all his life, he would take time out, if possible, during hunting season.

The Life I Love, C.S. Stobie

The largest collection of Schreyvogel canvases in existence today is located in the Thomas Gilcrease Institute of American History and Art in Tulsa, Oklahoma. "Custer's Demand" is there, along with such other favorites as "Through The Lines," "Attack At Dawn," and "The Duel."

A recent discovery of rare prints of Charles Schreyvogel's art work amidst the old files of the Buffalo Bill Memorial Museum, portray the spirit of the Old West. The gallery of eighteen large platinum prints inscribed by the artist around the turn of the century are one of the newest displays at the museum. It seems that the collection had been buried and literally forgotten by Baker and his successors after he founded the museum on Lookout Mountain in 1921. It comprises one of the largest collections of Charles Schreyvogel's work.

Schreyvogel (1861-1912) was a distinguished Western artist. Mild mannered and sickly, he was born January 4, 1861 of German immigrant parents — shopkeepers in lower east side New York. After some formal art instruction in Newark and lithographers' apprenticeship, he went abroad in 1886 to study in Munich, Germany. Little then did anyone realize that as an artist he would one day be written up by *Leslies Weekly* as *"The greatest living interpreter of the Old West"*.

After three years he returned to the United States and supported himself through commercial art work while longing to capture on canvas the winning of the West. The best he could afford was Buffalo Bill's Wild West Shows where he became well known to the troupe when they came east. Here he had the opportunity to sketch horses, cavalry charges, Cowboys and Indians.

In 1893, Schreyvogel's dream came true when he travelled west as a guest of Buffalo Bill and was able to visit many western regions. Most of that summer he spent in Colorado, sketching and collecting Indian and other frontier relics for his studio props so that his paintings would be historically accurate.

Later as a result of an invitation from President Teddy Roosevelt, Schreyvogel visited the many Indian reservations, forts and military encampments.

At first the resulting paintings did not sell. Not until 1899 after his painting *'My Bunkie'* was accepted did he eventually gain fame. That painting is now owned by the New York

Schreyvogel's is the classic story of the talented artist suffering — almost starving — before recognition of his greatness eased his hard life.

Schreyvogel at 40, was sufficiently mature to accept his sudden fame with equanimity, and his long struggle against poverty had virtually eliminated all trace of temperament.

Metropolitan Museum. This was the turning point in his life as he concentrated on Western historical paintings.

Each year Schreyvogel travelled across the west making preliminary sketches and photographs which he later used in his work.

It was during this period that the first platinum prints were made. This photographic process became extinct during World War I when platinum was declared a scarce metal. These delicate faithful reproductions are among the most beautiful produced in the history of photography, consisting of a deposit of platinum on specially prepared paper. Most of the prints have become unobtainable.

Paintings by Schreyvogel are also extremely rare. Most are in museums or special private collections. He was never a prolific painter and besides he died at the early age of 51. It is estimated that he painted less than 75 major canvases.

The Western paintings of Charles Schreyvogel, along with those of Remington and Russell, are today the foundation of any institutional collection of Western art.

While Remington's 3000 pictures and sculptures encompass virtually every phase of western life, and Russell's work deals principally with the cowboy. Charles Schreyvogel dedicated his entire career to capturing the Indian-fighting soldier. Schreyvogel's canvases, while large, are relatively few in number, but they possess qualities of color and draftsmanship seldom if ever demonstrated by either Russell or Remington.

Today, Charles Schreyvogel's work is gaining increased popular acclaim among collectors of Western art, and historians.

"The Duel."

Following Frederic Remington's death in 1909, Charles Schreyvogel was acclaimed by both the public and press as the logical heir to Remington's crown. In 1910, *Leslie's Illustrated Weekly* praised him as "America's greatest living interpreter of the Old West." This, unfortunately, was not to be for long. During the early winter of 1911-12, he became seriously infected. On January 27, 1912, he died a few days past his 51st birthday.

# POSTERS

Buffalo Bill's "Wild West" — the spectacular traveling show that portrayed incidents from Cody's life — had great influence on America's awareness of its western heritage.

Millions of people saw the show during its nearly 40 years on the road. But millions more saw the flamboyant, garish posters and billboards that were nailed or pasted to every available fence and wall to herald the arrival of the "Wild West."

"It is the thesis of this (Rennert's) book that the thousands of posters and billboards played a major part in the shaping of our image, tradition and romance of the American West."

It was the life of Buffalo Bill, and its re-enactment in the arena, which attracted the audience to the Wild West. So much of this attraction was Buffalo Bill himself and so much of the show was seen as a biographic rendering of his adventurous life — and what a life it was.

Buffalo Bill and his posters dramatized the West and made it real. The posters exploited a pageant of a passing era and Cody was well aware of it.

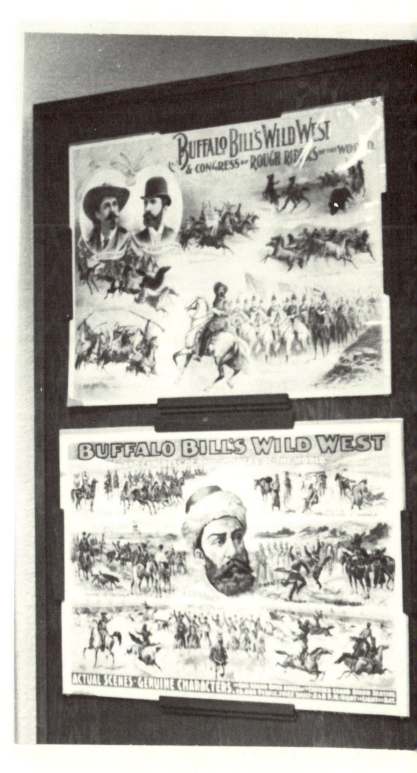

The extensive collection of Wild West Posters lends excitement to a lesson in our Western history. These priceless posters tell us an interesting chapter of a time gone by.

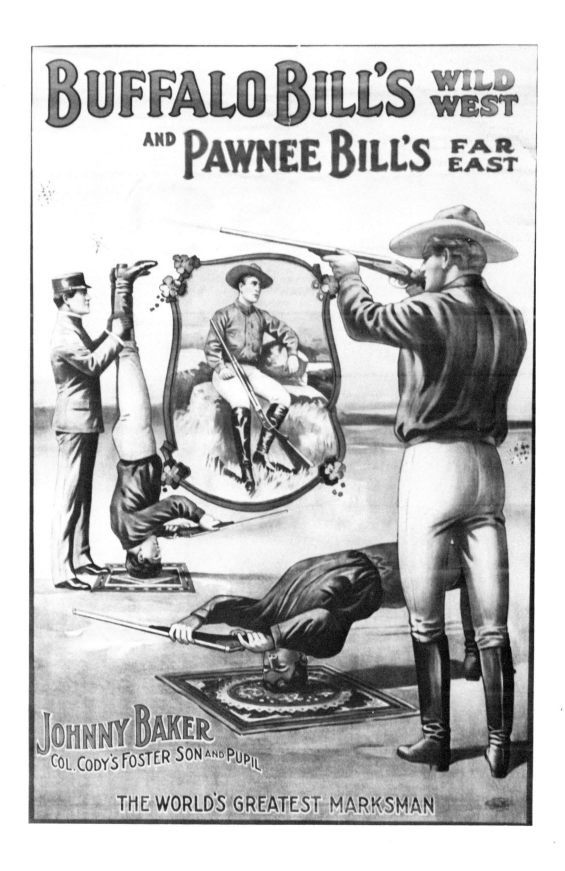

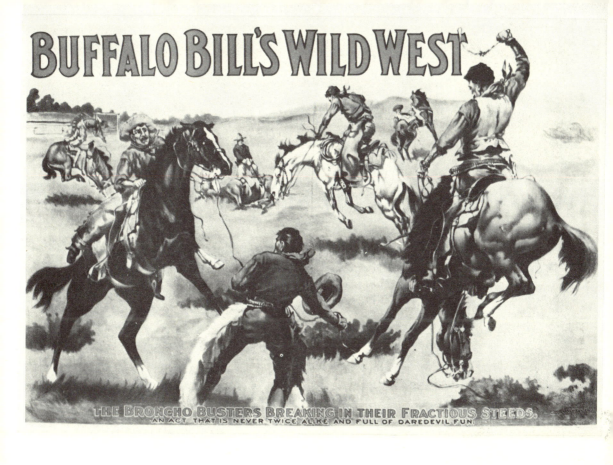

Ned Buntline did much to spread "Buffalo Bill's" fame through the "Dime Novels." The Dime Novels did not necessarily sell for ten cents. Some were a nickel, the thicker ones went for as high as twenty cents. Now they are collector's items. Tattered ones can bring a hundred dollars; mint condition specimens can bring thousands.

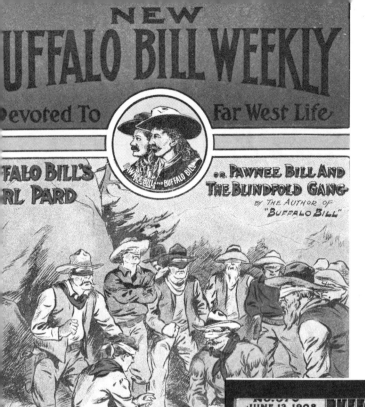

Not being wise in the way of finances he died penniless but rich in the love and devotion of respected friends. 25,000 people paid final tribute at the graveside on Lookout Mountain.

The body of Buffalo Bill Cody lay in state in the rotunda of the Colorado State Capital in Denver. It had been carried there on a horse drawn vehicle followed by his riderless horse, McKinley. On January 15th funeral services were held at the Denver Elk Club. His body was placed in a vault for final burial on June 3rd, 1917.

A dispute arose as to where the final resting place should be. Buffalo Bill had once expressed a desire to be buried atop Cedar Mountain near Cody, Wyoming, but a will that he had drawn up in New York in 1903 stated his wish to be interred in the mountains west of Denver, overlooking the plains that he so loved and were so much a part of his youth. Edgar McMechen, Curator of the State Historical Society confirmed that, "The Denver Post and especially Harry Tammen wanted to keep the body in the Denver area, and feared that the people of Cody would try to steal it." McMechen was asked to get Mrs. Louisa Cody's assurance that Buffalo Bill would be burried on Lookout Mountain. "For that assurance, I paid her $10,000."

At 1 p.m. on the day of burial, the casket was opened at the graveside, and 10,000 people marched by to witness and give last respects to their hero. The Hon. Col. William F. "Buffalo Bill" Cody was laid to his final rest on Lookout Mountain, overlooking *his* plains to the East. In spite of much controversy, he lies there today with his wife Louisa, who was buried with him in 1921.

# CHICAGO HERALD
## Fair and Square

THURSDAY MORNING, JANUARY 11, 1917.

# "BUFFALO BILL" IS DEAD

## 'BUFFALO BILL' DIES AFTER HARD FIGHT

### SCOUTS OF INDIAN DAYS END COMES JOIN WITH CHILDREN IN TO COL. CODY TRIBUTE TO FRONTIERSMAN AT SISTER'S DENVER HOME

## Buffalo Bill, Dead at 71, a Hero of Frontier Days
### Romance of the Great West in His Life Story

### IMPRESSIVE RITES AT CODY FUNERAL
Denver Pays Fitting Tribute to Empire Builder of the West

### 'Buffalo Bill' Cody Buried Atop Lookout Mountain
Visitors Come From Afar to See Grave of Famous Indian Fighter

### BUFFALO BILL CROSSES DIVIDE

### COL. CODY DIES IN BELOVED CITY; END IS PEACEFUL
Colonel Cody Dies Amid Civilization Where Once He Knew Wilds.

### TOM-TOMS WILL WAIL DIRGE OVER PRAIRIES FOR 'PAHASKA'S' DEATH
Passing of Buffalo Bill Will Be Mourned in Tepees Of Sioux as Breaking of Last Link With Old Wild West.

### FAMOUS SCOUT TO BE HONORED BY DENVER

### Buffalo Bill Rests In Peace—At Last

### HUNDREDS TRAVEL FAR TO PAY LAST TRIBUTE TO NOTED PLAINSMAN

### NOTED SCOUT LOSES LAST BATTLE

Buffalo Bill's funeral through the streets of Denver.

Cody's horse, "McKinley," during the funeral procession in June of 1917. Some people believe the horse used was not really McKinley, but a substitute provided by Tammen for publicity and effect.

The Lariat Trail to the Buffalo Bill grave and Museum atop Lookout Mountain. On this day a circus atmosphere prevailed as thousands of vehicles motored up Lariat Trail to the final resting place on Lookout Mountain.

The Colorado National Guard was called out to guard the grave in 1921, when word was received that a posse had left Cody, Wyoming with the intent of stealing Buffalo Bill's body. A severe storm blew in from the mountains and turned the posse back.

| | |
|---|---|
| **Born:** | February 26, 1846, near LeClaire, Scott County—eastern Iowa.<br>Father: Isaac Cody<br>Mother: Mary Ann Cody |
| 1854: | Moves to Kansas: Father takes up claim in Salt Creek Valley near Indian reservation and becomes an Indian trader. |
| 1854 to 1861: | Young Bill Cody is reared amidst trouble in which slaveholders and antislave men strove for political possession of Kansas. |
| 1857: | Is hired as extra or messenger boy for the Russel, Majors and Waddell bull train. Makes first trip to the plains. |
| 1857: | Freighter for Gen. Johnston's Army during the Morman War. Befriends "Wild Bill" Hickok. |
| 1858: | In the summer, becomes assistant wagon master with bull train bound for Fort Laramie. |
| 1859: | Attends school for nearly a month. |
| 1859: | Joins gold rush to Pikes Peak country in what is now Denver, Colorado. |
| 1859: | In the fall, joins a party of trappers on Chug Water River near Fort Laramie. |
| 1861: | Becomes a Pony Express rider: one of the youngest on the line at 14. Once rode 322 miles in 21 hours and 40 minutes exhausting 20 horses. |
| 1861 to 1863: | Although too young to enlist, he acts as ranger, dispatch bearer and scout in the service of the Union in Kansas and Missouri and on Santa Fe Trail. |
| 1864: | Following the death of his mother he enlists in Kansas Volunteer Infantry. Serves until war's end. |
| 1865 to 1866: | Works as stage driver between Fort Kearney, Nebraska, and Plum Creek, 35 miles west. |
| 1866: | Married March 6 to Louisa Frederci of St. Louis. |
| 1866: | Runs Golden Rule House Hotel at Salt Creek Valley, Kansas |
| 1866 to 1867: | Works as government scout at Fort Ellisworth, Fort Fletcher and Fort Hays, Kansas. Daughter Arta, born December 16, 1866. |
| 1867: | Promotes the town of Rome near Fort Hays. The venture fails. |
| 1867 to 1868: | Supplies Kansas Pacific Railroad with buffalo. Kills 4280 bison in 18 months. In a buffalo shooting tournament with a rival hunter he earns undisputed right to title: "Buffalo Bill." He earned $500 per month at the age of 21. |
| 1868: | Becomes government scout with headquarters at Fort Larned. Performs remarkable endurance rides between forts, once covering 355 miles in 58 hours of day and night riding. |
| 1868 to 1872: | Serves with Fifth Cavalry on various expeditions against Indians. |
| 1870: | Son, Kit Carson Cody, born November 26, 1870 and died in 1876 in Rochester, New York at the age of 5. |
| 1872: | Guides Grand Duke Alexis of Russia on a hunting trip. Elected to Nebraska Legislature on Democratic ticket at the age of 26. |
| 1872: | In August, Daughter, Orra, born. |
| 1872 to 1873: | Resigns from legislature and with Texas Jack goes east to act in Buntline's stage play. |
| 1874 to 1876: | Continues to be an actor, scout and guide. |
| 1876: | Rejoins Fifth Cavalry as scout against the Sioux. Following the Custer Massacre he fights his famous duel with Chief Yellow Hand. (Questionable) |
| 1877: | With Major Frank North establishes cattle ranch near North Platte, Nebraska. |
| 1876 to 1878: | Goes on theatrical tours portraying incidents from Sioux War. |
| 1878: | Establishes residence at North Platte, Nebraska. |
| 1882: | Organized a local celebration, "Old Glory Blowout" on July 4, in North Platte; now claimed to be the first organized rodeo in America. |
| 1883: | On February 9, 1883, daughter Irma, born. |
| 1883: | Organizes his Wild West Combination. Opens at Omaha, Nebraska, May 17. |

| | | | |
|---|---|---|---|
| 1883 to 1886: | Tours United States with Wild West Show. | 1900: | Bailey, of Barnum and Bailey, becomes his partner. |
| 1887: | Takes show on tour to England. | 1902: | Enlarged show again tours Europe. |
| 1889: | Takes show on tour of Continental Europe. | 1900 to 1910: | Pours money into various projects: irrigation systems, mines, etc., and finances friends and relatives. |
| 1889: | Is appointed Brigadier General of National Guard of Nebraska. | | |
| 1890: | Serves as chief of scouts under General Nelson A. Miles against the Sioux. | 1912: | Borrows money from Bonfils and Tammen of Denver pledging his services. |
| 1893: | Buffalo Bill's "Wild West" is a feature at World's Fair at Chicago. | 1913 to 1917: | Goes slowly downhill financially and dies January 10th at home of his sister, Mary Cody Decker at Denver, Colorado. He was buried on Lookout Mountain near Denver, Colorado just before his 71st birthday. |
| 1896: | Founds town of Cody, Wyoming. | | |
| 1898: | On August 31st, Cody's day celebrated in his honor at Omaha, Nebraska during trans-Missouri Exposition. | | |